Study Guide for the English to Speakers of Other Languages Test

▶ ▶ ▶ ▶ ▶ ▶ ▶ ▶ ▶ ▶ ▶ ▶

A PUBLICATION OF ETS

Table of Contents

Study Guide for the *English to Speakers of Other Languages* Test

▶   ▶   ▶   ▶   ▶   ▶   ▶   ▶   ▶   ▶   ▶   ▶

TABLE OF CONTENTS

Chapter 1

Chapter 2

Chapter 3

Chapter 4

Chapter 5

Chapter 6

Chapter 7

Appendix A

Appendix B

Chapter 1

**Introduction to the *English to Speakers of Other Languages*
Test and Suggestions for Using This Study Guide**

► ► ► ► ► ► ► ► ► ► ► ►

Introduction to the *English to Speakers of Other Languages* Test

The Praxis *English to Speakers of Other Languages* test is designed for prospective elementary and secondary teachers of English to speakers of other languages. The test is designed to measure the basic pedagogical knowledge necessary for a beginning teacher of ESOL in elementary or secondary schools.

Educational Testing Service® (ETS®) has aligned the questions on this test with the TESOL/NCATE *Standards for the Accreditation of Initial Programs in P–12 ESL Teacher Education* as developed by TESOL, Inc. ETS works in collaboration with teacher educators, higher education content specialists, and accomplished practicing teachers to keep the test updated and representative of current standards.

The *English to Speakers of Other Languages* test consists of 120 multiple-choice questions, with 20 questions based on recorded speech samples. The questions cover fundamental concepts that provide the foundation for teaching English to speakers of other languages. The questions test knowledge of essential facts, including the meanings of specific terms, understanding of relationships between and among areas of content, and the ability to apply concepts appropriately.

The content covered by the 120 questions is divided into the following categories:

Content Category	Number of Questions	Approximate Percentage of Examination
▪ Analysis of Student Language Production	30	25%
▪ Linguistic Theory	28	23%
▪ Teaching Methods and Techniques	36	30%
▪ Assessment Techniques and Cultural Issues	18	15%
▪ Professional Issues	8	7%

Test takers have 120 minutes to complete the test, which includes a 30-minute listening section.

The two sections of the test are broken down as indicated in the table below.

	Number of Questions	Time
Section I: Analysis of Student Language Production		
Part A: Oral Grammar and Vocabulary (Recorded portion of the test)	10	Approximately 15 minutes
Part B: Pronunciation (Recorded portion of the test)	10	Approximately 15 minutes
Part C: Writing	10	Approximately 10 minutes
Section II: Language Theory and Teaching	90	Approximately 80 minutes
TOTALS	120	120 minutes

The test is not intended to assess teaching skills but rather to demonstrate the test taker's fundamental knowledge in the major areas of the field of ESOL.

Suggestions for using the "Study Topics" chapter of this study guide

This test is different from a final exam or other tests you may have taken for other courses because it is comprehensive—that is, it covers material you may have learned in courses taken during your undergraduate or graduate program. It requires you to synthesize information you have learned from many sources and to understand the subject as a whole.

Therefore, you should review and prepare for the test rather than merely become familiar with the question formats. A thorough review of the material covered by the test will significantly increase your likelihood of success. Moreover, studying for your licensing exam is a great opportunity to reflect on and develop a deeper understanding of pedagogical knowledge and methods before you begin to teach, or to reflect on previous teaching experience. As you prepare to take the test, it may be particularly helpful for you to think about how you would apply the study topics and sample exercises to the classroom experience you obtained during your teacher-preparation program. Your student-teaching experience will be especially relevant to your thinking about the materials in the study guide.

We recommend the following approach for using the "Study Topics" chapter to prepare for the test:

- **Become familiar with the test content.** Learn what will be assessed in the test, covered in chapter 3.

- **Assess how well you know the content in each area.** After you learn what topics the test contains, you should assess your knowledge in each area. How well do you know the material? In which areas do you need to learn more before you take the test? It is quite likely that you will need to brush up on most or all of the areas.

- **Develop a study plan.** Assess what you need to study, and create a realistic plan for studying. You can develop your study plan in any way that works best for you. A "Study Plan" form is included in appendix A at the end of the book as a possible way to structure your planning. Remember that this is a licensure test and covers a great deal of material. Plan to review carefully. You will need to allow time to find the books and other materials, time to read the material and take notes, and time to go over your notes.

- **Identify study materials.** Most of the material covered by the test is contained in standard introductory textbooks for ESOL, linguistics, phonology, and related fields. If you do not own introductory texts that cover all the areas, you may want to borrow some from friends or from a library. You may also want to obtain a copy of state or national standards for ESOL. (One way to find these standards quickly is to go to the Web site for your state's Department of Education. You can also access the TESOL/NCATE *Standards for the Accreditation of Initial Programs in P–12 ESL Teacher Education* at www.TESOL.org.) Use standard school and college introductory textbooks and other reliable, professionally prepared materials. Don't rely heavily on information provided by friends or from searching the World Wide Web. Neither of these sources is as uniformly reliable as textbooks.

- **Work through your study plan.** You may want to work alone, or you may find it more helpful to work with a group or with a mentor. Work through the topics and questions provided in chapter 3. Rather than memorizing definitions from books, be able to define and discuss the topics in your own words and understand the relationships between diverse topics and concepts. If you are working with a group or mentor, you can also try informal quizzes and questioning techniques.

- **Read chapter 4.** This chapter will sharpen your skills in reading and answering multiple-choice questions. To succeed on multiple-choice questions, you must focus carefully on each question, avoid reading things into the question, pay attention to details, and sift patiently through the answer choices.

- **Proceed to the practice questions.** Once you have completed your review, you are ready to benefit from the "Practice Questions" portion of this guide.

Suggestions for using the "Practice Questions" and "Right Answers and Explanations" chapters

- **Answer the practice questions in chapter 5.** Work on the practice questions in a quiet place without distractions. Remember that the practice questions are only examples of the way the topics are covered in the test. The test will have different questions.

- **Score the practice questions.** Go through the detailed answers in chapter 6 ("Right Answers and Explanations") and mark the questions you answered correctly and the ones you missed. Look over the explanations of the questions you missed and see if you understand them.

- **Decide whether you need more review.** After you have looked at your results, decide whether there are areas that you need to brush up on before taking the actual test. Go back to your textbooks and reference materials to see if the topics are covered there. You might also want to go over your questions with a friend or teacher who is familiar with the subjects.

- **Assess your readiness.** Do you feel confident about your level of understanding in each of the areas? If not, where do you need more work? If you feel ready, complete the checklist in chapter 7 ("Are You Ready?") to double-check that you've thought through the details. If you need more information about registration or the testing situation itself, use the resources in appendix B: "For More Information."

Chapter 2
Background Information on The Praxis Series™ Assessments

▶ ▶ ▶ ▶ ▶ ▶ ▶ ▶ ▶ ▶ ▶ ▶

What Are The Praxis Series Subject Assessments?

The Praxis Series Subject Assessments are designed by ETS to assess your knowledge of specific subject areas. They are a part of the licensing procedure in many states. This study guide covers an assessment that tests your knowledge of the actual content you will be expected to teach once you are licensed. Your state has adopted The Praxis Series tests because it wants to confirm that you have achieved a specified level of mastery in your subject area before it grants you a license to teach in a classroom.

The Praxis Series tests are part of a national testing program, meaning that the test covered in this study guide is required in more than one state for licensure. The advantage of a national program is that if you want to move to another state, you can transfer your scores from one state to another. However, each state has specific test requirements and passing scores. If you are applying for a license in another state, you will want to verify the appropriate test and passing score requirements. This information is available online at www.ets.org/praxis/prxstate.html or by calling ETS at 800-772-9476 or 609-771-7395.

What Is Licensure?

Licensure in any area—medicine, law, architecture, accounting, cosmetology—is an assurance to the public that the person holding the license possesses sufficient knowledge and skills to perform important occupational activities safely and effectively. In the case of teacher licensing, a license tells the public that the individual has met predefined competency standards for beginning teaching practice.

Because a license makes such a serious claim about its holder, licensure tests are usually quite demanding. In some fields, licensure tests have more than one part and last for more than one day. Candidates for licensure in all fields plan intensive study as part of their professional preparation: some join study groups, others study alone. But preparing to take a licensure test is, in all cases, a professional activity. Because a licensure exam assesses the entire body of knowledge for the field you are entering, preparing for the test takes planning, discipline, and sustained effort.

Why Does My State Require The Praxis Series Assessments?

Your state chose The Praxis Series assessments because the tests assess the breadth and depth of content—called the "domain"—that your state wants its teachers to possess before they begin to teach. The level of content knowledge, reflected in the passing score, is based on recommendations of panels of teachers and teacher educators in each subject area. The state licensing agency and, in some states, the state legislature ratify the passing scores that have been recommended by panels of teachers.

What Do the Tests Measure?

The Praxis Series Subject Assessments are tests of content knowledge. They measure your understanding and skills in a particular subject area. Multiple-choice tests measure a broad range of knowledge across your content area. Constructed-response tests measure your ability to provide in-depth explanations of a few essential topics in a given subject area. Content-specific pedagogy tests, most of which are constructed response, measure your understanding of how to teach certain fundamental concepts in a subject area. The tests do not measure your actual teaching ability, however. They measure your knowledge of a subject and of how to teach it. The teachers in your field who help us design and write these tests, and the states that require them, do so in the belief that knowledge of your subject area is the first requirement for licensing. Teaching combines many complex skills, only some of which can be measured by a single test. While the test covered in this study guide measures content knowledge, your teaching ability is a skill that is typically measured in other ways—for example, through observation, videotaped practice, or portfolios.

How Were These Tests Developed?

ETS began the development of The Praxis Series Subject Assessments with a survey. For each subject, teachers around the country in various teaching situations were asked to judge which knowledge and skills a beginning teacher in that subject needs to possess. Professors in schools of education who prepare teachers were asked the same questions. These responses were ranked in order of importance and sent out to hundreds of teachers for review. All of the responses to these surveys (called "job analysis surveys") were analyzed to summarize the judgments of these professionals. From their consensus, we developed guidelines, or specifications, for the multiple-choice and constructed-response tests. Each subject area had a committee of practicing teachers and teacher educators who wrote the specifications, which were reviewed and eventually approved by teachers. From the test specifications, groups of teachers and professional test developers created test questions that met content requirements and satisfied the *ETS Standards for Quality and Fairness.**

When your state adopted The Praxis Series Subject Assessments, local panels of practicing teachers and teacher educators in each subject area met to examine the tests and to evaluate each question for its relevance to beginning teachers in your state. This is called a "validity study" because local practicing teachers validate that the test content is relevant to the job. For the test to be adopted in your state, teachers in your state must judge that it is valid. During the validity study, the panel also provides a passing-score recommendation. This process includes a rigorous review to determine how many of the test questions a beginning teacher in that state would be able to answer correctly. Your state's licensing agency then reviewed the panel's recommendations and made a final determination of the passing-score requirement.

Throughout the development process, practitioners in the field—teachers and teacher educators—participated in defining what The Praxis Series Subject Assessments would cover, which test would be used for licensure in your subject area, and what score would be needed to achieve licensure. This practice is consistent with how professional licensure works in most fields: those who are already licensed oversee the licensing of new practitioners. When you pass The Praxis Series Subject Assessments, you and the practitioners in your state will have evidence that you have the knowledge and skills required for beginning teaching practice.

---

* *ETS Standards for Quality and Fairness* (2003, Princeton, NJ) are consistent with the "Standards for Educational and Psychological Testing," industry standards issued jointly by the American Educational Research Association, the American Psychological Association, and the National Council on Measurement in Education (1999, Washington, DC).

Chapter 3
Study Topics

Introduction to the Test

The *English to Speakers of Other Languages* test assesses whether an examinee has the knowledge and competencies necessary for a beginning ESL teacher.

The topics for questions cover areas such as analysis of student language production, linguistic theory, teaching methods and techniques, assessment techniques, and cultural issues. The questions are designed to align with the TESOL/NCATE *Standards for the Accreditation of Initial Programs in P–12 ESL Teacher Education* published by Teachers of English to Speakers of Other Languages, Inc. (TESOL).

This chapter is intended to help you organize your preparation for the test and to give you a clear indication about the depth and breadth of the knowledge required for success on the test.

Here is an overview of the areas covered on the test, along with their subareas:

Analysis of Student Language Production
— Oral Grammar and Vocabulary
Pronunciation
Writing

Linguistic Theory
— Phonology
Morphology
Syntax
Psycholinguistics
Sociolinguistics

Teaching Methods and Techniques
— Identifying Methods
Selecting Methods
Determining Expectations
Differentiated Instruction
Classroom Management

Assessment Techniques and Cultural Issues
— Evaluation and Assessment
Cultural Issues

Professional Issues
— Curriculum and Materials
Programs and Models
Legal Foundations

Using the topic lists that follow

You are not expected to be an expert on all aspects of the topics that follow. You should understand the major characteristics of each topic, recognize the minor topics, and have some familiarity with the subtopics. Virtually all accredited ESL, TESL, ESOL, and TESOL teacher preparation programs address the majority of these topics, subtopics, and even minor topics.

You are likely to find that the topics below are covered by most introductory TESOL textbooks and textbooks for related fields (such as linguistics, phonology, teaching pronunciation, and teaching writing), but a general survey textbook may not cover all of the subtopics. Consult materials and resources, including lecture and laboratory notes, from all your TESOL course work. You should be able to match up specific topics and subtopics with what you have covered in your courses.

Try not to be overwhelmed by the volume and scope of content knowledge in this guide. An overview such as this, which lists topics in the field of ESL, does not offer you a great deal of context. Although a specific term may not seem familiar as you see it here, you might find you can understand it when the term is applied to a real-life situation. Many of the questions on the actual Praxis test will provide you with a context in which to apply these topics or terms, as you will see when you look at the practice questions in chapter 5.

Special questions marked with stars

Interspersed throughout the list of topics are questions that are outlined in boxes and preceded by stars (★). These questions are intended to help you test your knowledge of fundamental concepts and your ability to apply fundamental concepts to situations in the classroom or the real world. Most of the questions require you to combine several pieces of knowledge in order to formulate an integrated understanding and response. If you spend time on these questions, you will gain increased understanding and facility with the subject matter covered on the test. You might want to discuss these questions and your answers with a teacher or mentor.

Note that the questions marked with stars are not short answer or multiple choice and that this study guide does not provide the answers. The questions marked with stars are intended as study questions, not practice questions. Thinking about the answers to them should improve your understanding of fundamental concepts and will probably help you answer a broad range of questions on the test. For example, the following box with a star appears in the list of study topics under "Psycholinguistics":

> ★ What is interlanguage?

If you think about this question, perhaps by reviewing lecture notes or textbooks in the area of language acquisition, you probably will have prepared yourself to answer multiple-choice questions similar to the one below.

Which of the following best describes the concept of interlanguage?

(A) A categorization of sounds and words that second-language learners will find difficult to understand and acquire

(B) A plateau in language learning beyond which learners cannot proceed unless there is exceptional effort or motivation

(C) A developmental system based on first language, second-language input, language universals, and communication strategies

(D) A theory that proposes that all languages share common properties and that there is a hierarchy of stages of second-language acquisition that is not determined solely by the learner's first language

The correct answer is (C). Interlanguage is thought to be a system that language users use to make sense of a new language. This system is an "inter" language because it has unique qualities based on such things as the speaker's native language, language universals, and communication strategies.

Analysis of Student Language Production

Oral Grammar and Vocabulary, Pronunciation, Writing

As explained in the introduction, Section I of the test consists of samples of spoken and written English produced by ESOL students. Section I is divided into parts A, B, and C. Parts A and B are based on a recording that you will hear. In Part A, "Oral Grammar and Vocabulary," each excerpt will be played once. In Part B, "Pronunciation," the excerpts will be played twice. Be sure to listen to the excerpts carefully. As you listen, it's a good idea to mark up the transcript with observations about the speech sample (you can practice this when you take the practice test in chapter 5). The questions in Part C, "Writing," refer to excerpts from student compositions; therefore, Part C has no recording.

The topics described in the categories below go into more detail about the kind of knowledge you will need to answer the questions in Section I, "Analysis of Student Language Production," as well as Section II, "Language Theory and Teaching."

Linguistic Theory

Phonology

- Recognize similarities and differences between the phonologies of English and the languages of ESOL students

★ What sounds in English are typically problematic for speakers of various native languages?

- Understand how phonetic environment affects the pronunciation of individual sounds

★ What kinds of words most frequently occur in a reduced form in natural speech?

- Be familiar with intonation and stress patterns in English

★ What types of utterances have a rising intonation pattern?

★ What types of activities can help students identify word stress patterns in English?

- Be familiar with phonetic transcriptions of words and phrases

★ What are common phonetic transcriptions of the vowel sounds in North American English?

- Know how to apply knowledge of phonetics to help ESOL students

★ What types of activities can help ESOL students monitor and improve their proficiency in English pronunciation?

Morphology

- Recognize similarities and differences between the morphologies of English and the languages of ESOL students

★ Think of a language other than English with which you are familiar. Which affixes in English are comparable to affixes in this language?

- Understand how morphemes combine to create words in English

★ How does the addition of the suffix "-ly" affect the word "slow"?

★ What is the root of the word "unimaginable"?

- Be able to identify the stages of morphological development of ESOL learners

★ An ESOL student says, "I have two pen." Which English morpheme has the student not yet acquired?

■ Know how to help ESOL students develop strategies to learn new words and use their morphological knowledge of English to build vocabulary

★ How might a lesson on prefixes and suffixes help improve a student's ability to derive meaning from newly encountered words?

★ What kinds of activities would most likely help students use their knowledge of words to understand new words?

Syntax

■ Recognize similarities and differences between the syntactic systems of English and the languages of ESOL students

★ An ESOL student who is a native speaker of Spanish says, "I live in a house white." What is the most likely explanation for the occurrence of this error?

■ Be familiar with the major syntactic structures of English and know how ESOL students experience the stages of syntactic development

★ How are declarative sentences formed in English?

★ How are interrogative sentences formed in English?

★ What types of activities would most likely assist ESOL students in their development of English syntax?

■ Be able to identify the parts of speech, understand the English verb system, and analyze student errors

★ How does the word "treat" function differently in the following sentences?
Let me treat you to dinner.
Ice cream is a special treat.

★ What is the third person singular construction of the verb "write" in the present perfect tense?

■ Be familiar with idioms and nonliteral expressions and know how they can affect ESOL students' understanding of spoken and written English

★ What is an idiom?

★ How are idioms different from other nonliteral expressions?

★ What types of activities would most likely assist students in their understanding of nonliteral language use and idioms?

■ Understand how grammatical transformations and structural changes of sentences affect meaning

★ What are the grammatical differences between a sentence that uses the active voice and a sentence that uses the passive voice?

★ What are the grammatical differences between declarative and interrogative sentences?

■ Be familiar with theorists and theories of second-language acquisition

★ What are the significant aspects of Krashen's Natural Approach to second-language acquisition?

★ What are the differences between Basic Interpersonal Communication Skills (BICS) and Cognitive Academic Language Proficiency (CALP)?

★ Which theorist is associated with the theory of the "zone of proximal development"?

★ How does understanding of i+1 in theories of comprehensible input affect second-language instruction?

Psycholinguistics

- Be able to identify basic psycholinguistic concepts relating to second-language acquisition and classroom instruction

---

★ What is language interference?

★ What is interlanguage?

★ What psycholinguistic concept would be associated with the following student utterance: "I writed a letter yesterday"?

★ What types of errors do ESOL learners of particular native languages make due to negative transfer?

★ What is code-switching?

- Know how ESOL students progress through the stages of second-language development and understand how to help them at each stage

---

★ What is a "silent period" in an ESOL student's language development and what are some activities that accommodate a student in this stage?

★ What is the typical sequence that ESOL students follow in the acquisition of morphemes?

- Understand how student motivation and affective environment can affect second-language acquisition

---

★ What is the difference between instrumental motivation and integrative motivation?

★ What types of activities are most likely to lower an ESOL student's affective filter?

- Understand how different learning styles can affect second-language acquisition

---

★ What kinds of activities are best suited for kinesthetic learning?

★ How do learners who are adept visual learners process information?

Sociolinguistics

- Be able to identify sociolinguistic concepts relating to language learning and classroom instruction

---

★ What do the following terms mean: communicative competence, proxemics, semantics?

★ What types of activities give ESOL students practice using different registers?

- Be able to understand what nonstandard dialects are and why they are not considered markers of intellectual ability

---

★ What are World Englishes?

Teaching Methods and Techniques

Identifying and Selecting Methods

- Be able to identify and compare second-language instructional methods

---

★ What is Total Physical Response?

★ What is the Natural Approach to language learning?

★ How does the Direct Method of language instruction differ from the Audiolingual Method?

★ What types of activities are most effective in teaching receptive skills and productive skills?

- Understand the connection between instructional methods and language-acquisition theories

★ How does the theory of comprehensible input support the Total Physical Response technique?

★ What is the relationship between CALLA (Cognitive Academic Language Learning Approach) and Cummins' CALP?

★ How does Krashen's Natural Approach support communicative-based instruction?

Determining Expectations, Differentiated Instruction, Classroom Management

- Be able to identify instructional methods appropriate for ESOL students with a wide range in proficiency

★ What types of instructional techniques would be most effective with port-of-entry ESOL students?

★ What kinds of skills would be most important for a teacher to focus on with a group of ESOL students who are almost ready to transition into mainstream English classes?

★ How do appropriate methods of correction vary when a teacher is dealing with beginner ESOL students, as compared to advanced ESOL students?

★ How does amount of schooling in an ESOL student's native language affect second-language acquisition?

★ How do techniques differ for teaching second languages to students who are literate versus illiterate in their native languages?

Assessment Techniques and Cultural Issues

Evaluation and Assessment

- Be able to judge the appropriateness of assessments for skills targeted for testing

★ What kinds of tests best focus on ESOL students' comprehension skills?

★ How might vastly different scores achieved by the same ESOL student on the same test material be explained?

★ How can language-proficiency skills affect the outcome of an assessment of cognitive achievement?

★ How can cultural bias affect the scores of ESOL students on standardized tests?

- Be able to identify appropriate criteria for determining ESOL students' status and placement

★ What factors determine a student's candidacy for an ESOL program?

★ What criteria should be used to determine whether an ESOL student is ready to be exited from an ESOL program?

★ How do special education needs factor into decisions about placing an ESOL student?

★ What important factors contribute to the decision to advance an ESOL student to the next level of instruction or retain the student for further instruction at the current level?

Cultural Issues

- Be able to recognize the nature, role, and content of culture as it relates to language development and academic achievement

- Be able to recognize ways in which cultural variables affect second-language acquisition and teaching

- Be able to recognize the role of nonverbal communication within ESL instruction

★ What is ethnocentrism?

★ How does the role of family vary between cultures and how might this affect language acquisition?

★ How does the student-teacher relationship vary between cultures and what kinds of misunderstandings might the differences create?

★ How does eye contact vary between cultures?

★ What information about cultural differences might be useful to a content-area teacher who is teaching ESOL students?

Professional Issues

Curriculum and Materials

- Be able to recognize different types of curriculum design and the intended purpose of each

★ What is English for Special Purposes and what types of ESOL students are most likely to benefit from this design?

★ What is the role of English language skill development in content-area classes?

★ What types of curricula would most likely benefit English-language learners with specific career goals?

- Know how to select materials appropriate for students at specific language-proficiency levels

★ What types of texts are most effective with beginning ESOL students?

★ How can content-area materials be adapted for ESOL students?

★ What types of supplemental materials are appropriate for ESOL students at specific levels?

- Be familiar with acronyms of the ESL field

★ What is TESOL and what types of requirements are included in the TESOL standards for ESOL students?

★ What do common ESL acronyms, such as EFL, ELL, NABE, and LEP, mean?

Programs and Models

- Be able to identify different ESL program models and demonstrate understanding of their implementation

★ What is ESL pullout?

★ What are the characteristics of a sheltered ESL class?

★ How are dual-immersion programs implemented?

★ What are the advantages and disadvantages of ESL immersion programs?

★ What are the advantages and disadvantages of bilingual programs?

Legal Foundations

- Recognize the ways in which federal and state regulations influence programs for English-language learners and the implementation of programs in schools

★ What does *Lau* v. *Nichols* state and how does it affect ESL programs in all schools?

★ How does the No Child Left Behind Act affect the reporting of ESOL students' scores on standardized tests?

Chapter 4

Succeeding on Multiple-Choice Questions

▶ ▶ ▶ ▶ ▶ ▶ ▶ ▶ ▶ ▶ ▶ ▶ ▶

Why Multiple-Choice Tests Take Time

When you take the practice test in chapter 5, you will see that there are very few simple identification questions of the sort that ask, "Which of the following books on language development did Noam Chomsky write?" When The Praxis Series assessments were first being developed by professionals and postsecondary educators across the country, it was almost unanimously agreed that prospective school teachers should be able to analyze situations, synthesize material, and apply knowledge to specific examples. In short, they should be able to think as well as to recall specific facts, figures, or formulas. Consequently, you will find that you are being asked to think and to solve problems on these tests. Such activity takes more time than responding to questions requiring you to identify simple facts.

In addition, questions that require you to analyze situations, synthesize material, and apply knowledge are usually longer than are simple identification questions. The Praxis Series test questions often present you with something to read (a language sample, a sample of student work, or a brief teaching scenario) and then ask you questions based on your reading. Strong reading skills are required, and you must read carefully. Both on this test and as an education professional, you will need to process and use what you read efficiently.

If you know that your reading skills are not strong, you may want to take a reading course. College campuses have reading labs that can help you strengthen your reading skills.

Understanding Multiple-Choice Questions

When you read multiple-choice questions on the *English to Speakers of Other Languages* test, you will probably notice that the syntax (word order) is different from the word order you're used to seeing in ordinary material that you read, such as newspapers or textbooks. One of the reasons for this difference is that many test questions contain the phrase "which of the following."

To answer a multiple-choice question successfully, you need to consider carefully the context set up by the question and limit your choice of answers to the list given. The purpose of the phrase "which of the following" is to remind you to do this. For example, look at this question.

Which of the following is a flavor made from beans?

(A)   Strawberry
(B)   Cherry
(C)   Vanilla
(D)   Mint

You may know that chocolate and coffee are also flavors made from beans, but they are not listed, and the question asks you to select from the list that follows ("which of the following"). So the answer has to be the only bean-derived flavor in the list: vanilla.

Notice that the answer can be substituted for the phrase "which of the following." In the question above, you could insert "vanilla" for "which of the following" and have the sentence "Vanilla is a flavor made from beans." Sometimes it helps to cross out "which of the following" and insert the various choices. You may want to give this technique a try as you answer various multiple-choice questions on the practice test.

Looking carefully at the "which of the following" phrase helps you to focus on what the question is asking you to find and on the answer choices. In the simple example above, all of the answer choices are flavors. Your job is to decide which of the flavors is the one made from beans.

The vanilla bean question is pretty straightforward. But the phrase "which of the following" can also be found in more challenging questions. Look at this question.

> Which of the following teacher actions would best support the development of the literacy skills of elementary ESOL students?
>
> (A)   Using a commercially developed mainstream language-arts curriculum aligned with national standards
> (B)   Creating attractive bulletin boards using commercially prepared materials
> (C)   Teaching phonics, decoding, and word-recognition skills using mainstream grade-level work sheets
> (D)   Providing students with motivating reading and writing materials and assignments at an appropriate level

The placement of "which of the following" tells you that the list of choices is a list of teacher actions (in this case, these are examples of things a teacher might do with a group of elementary ESOL students). What are you supposed to find as an answer? You are supposed to find the choice that best supports the development of literacy skills.

Sometimes it helps to put the question in your own words. Here, you could paraphrase the question as "Which of these activities would best help students develop literacy skills?" The correct answer is (D). (Research has found that motivating reading materials and assignments at an appropriate level are the most effective for literacy development.)

You may also find that it helps to circle or underline each of the critical details of the question in your test book so you don't miss any of them.

> Which of the following teacher actions would best support the development of literacy skills of elementary ESOL students?

It is only by looking at all parts of the question carefully that you will have all of the information you need to answer it. With enough practice you should be able to figure out what any question is asking. Knowing the answer is, of course, a different matter, but you have to understand a question before you can answer it correctly.

It takes more work to understand "which of the following" questions when there are even more words in a question. Questions that require application or interpretation usually require more reading than straight naming-the-activity questions would.

Consider this question.

Question 1 refers to the following section of a table of contents in an ESOL textbook.

CONTENTS

Lesson 1 **Try Our Special Offer** . . . . **Page 1**

    WHAT: to describe specific people and things; to give reasons; to emphasize; to show uncertainty

    HOW: relative clauses

Lesson 2 **An "Excellent Opportunity"** . . . . **Page 8**

    WHAT: to read an ad; to write a letter of application

    HOW: paragraph construction

Lesson 3 **Buying a Computer** . . . . **Page 35**

    WHAT: to discuss the future; to read ads; to describe features of a computer; to use some language of contemporary technology

    HOW: collective nouns; "the" with plural and mass nouns; "the" with the names of places

---

1. This ESOL textbook uses which of the following organizational patterns?

    (A)   Hierarchical
    (B)   Grammatical
    (C)   Notional-functional
    (D)   Core

Given the placement of the phrase "which of the following," you can see that the list of answer choices is a list of "patterns." You are supposed to pick the pattern that best matches the information presented in the excerpted table of contents.

Being able to select the right answer depends on your understanding of the different ways that instructional materials are organized for ESOL students. Although some component parts of the patterns represented by choices (A), (B), and (D) may be contained in this table of contents, the focus of the text is on notional-functional patterns. Lesson headings like "Buying a Computer" should alert you to the fact that function is the organizing factor and lead you to the answer of (C).

Understanding Questions Containing "NOT," "LEAST," or "EXCEPT"

The words NOT, LEAST, and EXCEPT can make comprehension of test questions more difficult. Such questions ask you to select the choice that doesn't fit, or that is different in some specified way from the other answer choices. You must be very careful with this question type because it's easy to forget that you're selecting the negative. This question type is used in situations in which there are several good solutions, or ways to approach something, but also a clearly wrong way. These words are either capitalized or italicized when they appear in Praxis test questions, but they are easily (and frequently) overlooked.

For the following test question, determine what kind of answer you're looking for and what the details of the question are.

Which of the underlined words in the sentence below is NOT a relative pronoun?

<u>That</u> is the dog <u>that</u> chases the cat <u>that</u> lives in the
  A   B   C

house <u>that</u> Lois built.
      D

To answer this question, you have to determine which of the four choices is NOT a relative pronoun. In choices (B), (C), and (D), "that" is a relative pronoun, whereas the "that" in choice (A) is a demonstrative pronoun. Therefore, (A) is the correct answer.

TIP

It's easy to get confused while you're processing the information to answer a question with a "NOT," "LEAST," or "EXCEPT" in the question. If you treat the word "NOT" as one of the details you must satisfy, you have a better chance of understanding what the question is asking. And when you check your answer, make "NOT" one of the details you check for.

Be Familiar with Multiple-Choice Question Types

You will probably see more than one question format on a multiple-choice test. Here are examples of some of the more common question formats.

1. Questions with recorded and written excerpts

This type of question begins with a recorded speech sample or written excerpt from a nonnative English speaker. Each of the recorded speech samples is printed in your test book. Following the speech sample or written excerpt is a question that asks you to, for example, analyze aspects of the sample, reflect on a trend, or select an appropriate instructional activity to address aspects of the sample.

Consider this question.

Recorded speech sample:

She was very tired at the end of the day. (Student pronounces "she" as [si].)

The error in pronunciation in the word "she" indicates a problem with

(A)   intonation patterns
(B)   points of articulation
(C)   voiced and voiceless sounds
(D)   word stress patterns

Initial consonant forms are not influenced by stress and intonation, and [s] and [ʃ] are both voiceless sounds. However, the place of articulation of these two sounds is different: [s] is an alveolar fricative sound, or a sound that is produced with the tip of the tongue on or near the tooth ridge, and [ʃ] is a palato-alveolar fricative sound, or a sound that is produced with the tongue farther back in the mouth. Therefore, (B) is the correct answer.

2. Complete the statement

In this type of question, you are given an incomplete statement. You must select the choice that will make the completed statement correct. Look at the following example.

An appropriate way to determine a new ESOL student's level for classroom placement would be to

(A)   ask other teachers who have spoken with the student
(B)   ask the student in which level he or she feels most comfortable
(C)   administer a diagnostic test
(D)   administer an achievement test

To check your answer, reread the question and add your answer choice at the end. Be sure that your choice best completes the sentence. The correct answer is (C).

3. Which of the following

This question type is discussed in detail in a previous section. Also discussed above are strategies for helping you understand what the question is asking and for understanding details in the question that will help you select the correct choice. Consider this additional example.

Which of the following groups contains three words that are pronounced differently depending on whether they are used as nouns or verbs?

(A)   Lick, bottle, can
(B)   Table, herd, carpet
(C)   Drive, catalog, board
(D)   Sow, entrance, present

This question asks you to choose the group of words that are pronounced one way when they are used as nouns and another way when they are used as verbs. Pronounce these words to yourself to check your answer. The correct answer is (D).

4. Roman numeral choices

This format is used when there can be more than one correct answer in the list. Consider the following example.

Of the sentences below, which two contain a weak reference?

I.   The teacher disapproved of the students' wearing shorts in school.
II. We spent the whole day on a bird-watching expedition, but we didn't see one.
III. José found time for his composing whenever he could, but none of his music was ever published.
IV. He was an excellent horseman, but he never owned any.

(A)   I and III
(B)   I and IV
(C)   II and III
(D)   II and IV

One useful strategy in this type of question is to assess each possible answer before looking at the answer choices. Then evaluate the answer choices. In the question above, sentence II and sentence IV contain weak references (a "weak reference" is a grammatical term that describes a situation in which a pronoun used in a sentence is not clearly linked to the noun to which the pronoun is supposed to refer). The correct answer is (D).

5. Questions containing NOT, LEAST, EXCEPT

This question type is discussed at length above. It asks you to select the choice that doesn't fit. You must be very careful with this question type because it's easy to forget that you're selecting the negative. This question type is used in situations in which there are several good solutions, or ways to approach something, but also a clearly wrong way to do something.

6. Questions with graphics, tables, or scenarios

The important thing to keep in mind when answering questions about graphics, tables, or scenarios is to answer the question that is asked. In the case of a graphic or a table, you should consider reading the question first, and then look at the graphic or table in light of the question you have to answer. In the case of a scenario, you might want to go ahead and read the scenario, marking places you think are important, and then read the question.

7. Other formats

New formats are developed from time to time in order to find new ways of assessing knowledge with multiple-choice questions. If you see a format you are not familiar with, read the directions carefully. Then read and approach the question the way you would any other question, asking yourself what you are supposed to be looking for and what details are given in the question that can help you find the answer.

Useful Facts about the *English to Speakers of Other Languages* Test

1. You can answer Section I, Part C, and Section II of the test in any order. Section I, Parts A and B, consists of questions based on recorded excerpts. You are not able to go back to Section I, Parts A and B, after you have listened to the recording. For Section I, Part C, and for Section II of the test, you can go through the questions in order, as many test takers do, or you can create your own path. Perhaps you will want to answer questions in your strongest area first and then move from your strengths to your weaker areas. There is no right or wrong way. Use the approach that works for you.

2. There are no trick questions on the test. You don't have to find any hidden meanings or worry about trick wording. All of the questions on the test ask about subject-matter knowledge in a straightforward manner.

3. Don't worry about answer patterns. There is one myth that says that answers on multiple-choice tests follow patterns. There is another myth that there will never be more than two questions with the same lettered answer following each other. There is no truth to either of these myths. Select the answer you think is correct, based on your knowledge of the subject.

4. There is no penalty for guessing. Your test score is based on the number of correct answers you have, and incorrect answers are not counted against you. When you don't know the answer to a question, try to eliminate any obviously wrong answers and then guess at the correct one.

5. It's OK to write in your test book. You can work problems right on the pages of the book, make notes to yourself, mark questions you want to review later, or write anything at all. Your test book will be destroyed after you are finished with it, so use it in any way that is helpful to you.

Smart Tips for Taking the Test

1. Put your answers in the right "bubbles." It seems obvious, but be sure that you are "bubbling in" the answer to the right question on your answer sheet. A surprising number of examinees fill in a bubble without checking to see that the number matches the question they are answering.

2. Skip the questions you find to be extremely difficult. There are sure to be some questions that you think are hard. Rather than trying to answer these on your first pass through the test, leave them blank and mark them in your test book so you can come back to them. Pay attention to the time as you answer the rest of the questions on the test and try to finish with 10 or 15 minutes remaining so that you can go back over the questions you left blank. Even if you don't know the answers the second time you read the questions, see if you can narrow down the possible answers, and then guess.

3. Keep track of the time. Take a watch to the test, just in case the clock in the test room is difficult for you to see. On average, you have about one minute to answer each of the multiple-choice questions. One minute may not seem like much time, but you will be able to answer a number of questions in only a few seconds each. You will probably have plenty of time to answer all of the questions, but if you find yourself becoming bogged down in one section, you may decide to move on and come back to that section later.

4. Read all of the possible answers before selecting one—and then reread the question to be sure the answer you have selected really answers the question being asked. Remember that a question that contains a phrase like "Which of the following does NOT…" is asking for the one answer that is NOT a correct statement or conclusion.

5. Check your answers. If you have extra time left over at the end of the test, look over each question and make sure that you have filled in the bubble on the answer sheet as you intended. Many examinees make careless mistakes that could have been corrected if they had checked their answers.

6. Don't worry about your score when you are taking the test. No one is expected to get all of the questions correct. Your score on this test is not similar to your score on the SAT, the GRE, or other similar tests. It does not matter on this test whether you score very high or barely pass. If you meet the minimum passing score for your state and you meet the other requirements of the state for obtaining a teaching license, you will receive a license.

Chapter 5

Practice Questions

▶ ▶ ▶ ▶ ▶ ▶ ▶ ▶ ▶ ▶ ▶ ▶ ▶ ▶

Now that you have studied the content topics and have worked through strategies related to multiple-choice questions, you should take the following practice test. You will probably find it helpful to simulate actual testing conditions, giving yourself about 90 minutes to work on the questions. You can cut out and use the answer sheet provided if you wish.

When you are ready to start the test, start playing the CD on a stereo or portable CD player. The CD will guide you through Section I of the practice administration—let it run, and it will present the short speeches you need to listen to for questions 1 through 15.

Keep in mind that the test you take at an actual administration will have different questions, although the proportion of questions in each area and major subarea will be approximately the same. You should not expect the percentage of questions you answer correctly on the practice test to be exactly the same as when you take the test at an actual administration, since numerous factors affect a person's performance in any given testing situation.

When you have finished the practice questions, you can score your answers and read the explanations of the best answer choices in chapter 6.

THE PRAXIS
S E R I E S
Professional Assessments for Beginning Teachers ®

TEST NAME:

English to Speakers
of Other Languages (0360)

90 Practice Questions

Time—90 Minutes

90 Multiple-Choice Questions

(Note: At the official test administration, there will be 120 multiple-choice questions and you will be allowed 120 minutes to complete the test.)

(ETS)

THE **PRAXIS** S E R I E S ™

Answer Sheet C

DO NOT USE INK

Use only a pencil with soft black lead (No. 2 or HB) to complete this answer sheet.
Be sure to fill in completely the oval that corresponds to the proper letter or number.
Completely erase any errors or stray marks.

1. NAME
Enter your last name and first initial.
Omit spaces, hyphens, apostrophes, etc.

F I

Last Name
(first 6 letters)

2.

YOUR NAME:
(Print)

Last Name (Family or Surname)   First Name (Given)   M.I.

MAILING ADDRESS:
(Print)

P.O. Box or Street Address   Apt. # (If any)

City   State or Province

Country   Zip or Postal Code

TELEPHONE NUMBER: (   )   (   )
Home   Business

SIGNATURE: **TEST DATE:**

3. DATE OF BIRTH

Month	Day
Jan.	
Feb.	
Mar.	
April	
May	
June	
July	
Aug.	
Sept.	
Oct.	
Nov.	
Dec.	

4. SOCIAL SECURITY NUMBER

5. CANDIDATE ID NUMBER

6. TEST CENTER / REPORTING LOCATION

Center Number   Room Number

Center Name

City   State or Province

Country

7. TEST CODE / FORM CODE

0
1

8. TEST BOOK SERIAL NUMBER

9. TEST FORM

10. TEST NAME

MH04167   Q2573-06   51055 • 08920 • TF74E400

202974

1 2 3 4

BE SURE EACH MARK IS DARK AND COMPLETELY FILLS THE INTENDED SPACE AS ILLUSTRATED HERE: ● .

#		#		#		#	
1	A B C D	41	A B C D	81	A B C D	121	A B C D
2	A B C D	42	A B C D	82	A B C D	122	A B C D
3	A B C D	43	A B C D	83	A B C D	123	A B C D
4	A B C D	44	A B C D	84	A B C D	124	A B C D
5	A B C D	45	A B C D	85	A B C D	125	A B C D
6	A B C D	46	A B C D	86	A B C D	126	A B C D
7	A B C D	47	A B C D	87	A B C D	127	A B C D
8	A B C D	48	A B C D	88	A B C D	128	A B C D
9	A B C D	49	A B C D	89	A B C D	129	A B C D
10	A B C D	50	A B C D	90	A B C D	130	A B C D
11	A B C D	51	A B C D	91	A B C D	131	A B C D
12	A B C D	52	A B C D	92	A B C D	132	A B C D
13	A B C D	53	A B C D	93	A B C D	133	A B C D
14	A B C D	54	A B C D	94	A B C D	134	A B C D
15	A B C D	55	A B C D	95	A B C D	135	A B C D
16	A B C D	56	A B C D	96	A B C D	136	A B C D
17	A B C D	57	A B C D	97	A B C D	137	A B C D
18	A B C D	58	A B C D	98	A B C D	138	A B C D
19	A B C D	59	A B C D	99	A B C D	139	A B C D
20	A B C D	60	A B C D	100	A B C D	140	A B C D
21	A B C D	61	A B C D	101	A B C D	141	A B C D
22	A B C D	62	A B C D	102	A B C D	142	A B C D
23	A B C D	63	A B C D	103	A B C D	143	A B C D
24	A B C D	64	A B C D	104	A B C D	144	A B C D
25	A B C D	65	A B C D	105	A B C D	145	A B C D
26	A B C D	66	A B C D	106	A B C D	146	A B C D
27	A B C D	67	A B C D	107	A B C D	147	A B C D
28	A B C D	68	A B C D	108	A B C D	148	A B C D
29	A B C D	69	A B C D	109	A B C D	149	A B C D
30	A B C D	70	A B C D	110	A B C D	150	A B C D
31	A B C D	71	A B C D	111	A B C D	151	A B C D
32	A B C D	72	A B C D	112	A B C D	152	A B C D
33	A B C D	73	A B C D	113	A B C D	153	A B C D
34	A B C D	74	A B C D	114	A B C D	154	A B C D
35	A B C D	75	A B C D	115	A B C D	155	A B C D
36	A B C D	76	A B C D	116	A B C D	156	A B C D
37	A B C D	77	A B C D	117	A B C D	157	A B C D
38	A B C D	78	A B C D	118	A B C D	158	A B C D
39	A B C D	79	A B C D	119	A B C D	159	A B C D
40	A B C D	80	A B C D	120	A B C D	160	A B C D

FOR ETS USE ONLY | R1 | R2 | R3 | R4 | R5 | R6 | R7 | R8 | TR | CS

ENGLISH TO SPEAKERS OF OTHER LANGUAGES

Section I: Analysis of Student Language Production

Part A

Oral Grammar and Vocabulary
Approximate time—10 minutes

Directions: In this part of the test you will hear a series of short speeches by nonnative speakers of English. The recording will progress as follows.

First, you will hear a short recording of a student of English as a second language. To help you remember what you hear, a transcript of the recording is printed in your test book. After you listen to the student's speech, you will be asked to read and answer questions about the student's problems in grammar or vocabulary as evidenced by the speech. Time will be allotted for you to choose your answers and mark them on your answer sheet.

It is strongly suggested that you make notes on the printed transcripts as you listen to the recordings.

Example

Listen to the following student as she answers a question in class. The teacher has just asked her why she looks tired.

You will hear and read: "Because I go to bed late last night."

Now read the sample question.

The student's sentence contains an error in

(A) tense
(B) number
(C) person
(D) gender

Sample Answer

Ⓐ ● Ⓒ Ⓓ

The best answer is (A), "tense." Therefore, you would mark (A) on your answer sheet.

Now let us begin the test with the first nonnative speaker.

For Question 1, listen as a student talks about his brother.

The same, like, he's the same tall like me, but he looks, like, older.

1. The error in the student's statement involves the use of which of the following?

   (A) Figurative language
   (B) Superlative adjectives
   (C) Relative clauses
   (D) Comparative structures

For Question 2, listen as a student describes his hobby.

Oh, I love computers. Uh… I like to play games, like, to go Internet, search about the computers, all the computer stuff, I love it.

2. Which of the following occurs in this speech sample?

   (A) A preposition is missing.
   (B) An adverb is placed incorrectly.
   (C) A pronoun is missing an antecedent.
   (D) An unnecessary conjunction is added.

For Questions 3 and 4, listen as a student talks about visiting the United States.

I coming, I coming here <u>when I have twelve years</u>. I coming for eight months, came for, for eight, for, sorry, for eight months, uh…

3. In the speech sample, the student most likely is intending to do which of the following?

   (A) Talk about two events that took place in the recent past
   (B) Talk about how old he was at a given time in the past
   (C) Relate how long he plans to stay in the United States
   (D) Relate how old he will be after a certain period of time

4. The underlined phrase is most likely the result of

   (A) code-switching
   (B) negative transfer
   (C) avoidance
   (D) displacement

For Question 5, listen as a speaker describes what he saw inside his computer.

And, um, it was so cool inside, it's so cool, you see, like a little microchip and it's like so small and you think, how it can works?

5. In the final phrase, the student demonstrates difficulty with which of the following?

   (A) Register
   (B) Question formation
   (C) Pronoun reference
   (D) Preposition placement

For Question 6, listen as a student talks about her free time.

Well, I like to read and practice sports and . . . I like to . . . to keep bus-bus-busy.

6. The student's repetition of "busy" is an example of which of the following?

    (A)   A dialectal variation
    (B)   A coined phrase
    (C)   A self-correction
    (D)   Poetic language

For Question 7, listen as a student describes his first impression of the United States.

I was surprised because too much people, eh, the, the, em, highways and <u>roads too bigs</u> and too much cars and the houses too big, and, too big this country.

7. The underlined phrase demonstrates an error in the use of

    (A)   adjectives
    (B)   pronouns
    (C)   coordination
    (D)   tense

Section I: Analysis of Student Language Production

Part B: Pronunciation

Approximate time—10 minutes

Directions: In this part of the test you will listen to more speeches by nonnative speakers of English. The recording will continue as follows.

First, you will hear a short speech. To help you remember what you heard, a transcript of the recording will be printed in your test book. Then you will read a question about one of the student's problems in pronunciation as evidenced in the speech. You will NOT be asked to evaluate the student's grammar or vocabulary usage. To help you answer each pronunciation question, the recorded speech will be played a second time. Then you will be asked to answer the question. Time will be allotted for you to choose your answer to each question and mark it on your answer sheet.

It is strongly suggested that you make notes on the printed transcripts as you listen to the recordings.

Example

Listen to the following student as she answers a question in class. The teacher has just asked her why she looks tired.

You will hear and read: "Because I went to bed late last night."

Now read the sample question.

The student pronounces the word "went" in which of the following ways?

(A)   [wɛnt]
(B)   [vɛnt]
(C)   [vɑnt]
(D)   [wunt]

> **Sample Answer**
> Ⓐ ● Ⓒ Ⓓ

Now listen again. "Because I went to bed late last night."

The best answer is (B), "[vɛnt]." Therefore, you would mark (B) on your answer sheet.

For Question 8, listen as a student reads from a passage about bananas.

People started eating bananas thousands of years ago. Scientists who study plants think this fruit first grew in Asia.

8. The student is having the most difficulty producing which of the following sounds?

   (A)   Initial [θ]
   (B)   Initial [f]
   (C)   Initial [s]
   (D)   Final [s]

For Question 9, listen as a student reads from a passage about the Sun.

The Sun starts every shadow. The Sun is very <u>bright</u>. It shines on the house. It shines on the trees. It shines on you.

9. As pronounced by the student, the underlined word contains the sound

   (A)   [t]
   (B)   [p]
   (C)   [g]
   (D)   [ŋ]

For Question 10, listen as a student reads from a passage about insects.

Bees are furry <u>insects</u> with six legs.

10. In the underlined word, the student demonstrates difficulty with which of the following?

   (A)   Consonant clusters
   (B)   Vowels in initial position
   (C)   Voiceless consonants in final position
   (D)   Word stress

For Question 11, listen as a student reads from a passage about teeth.

You might think that your bones are the hardest parts, but they're not. The answer is—your teeth! Bone is very hard, but it would wear down after many years of <u>cutting</u> and chewing.

11. Which of the following best characterizes the student's pronunciation of the "t" sound in the underlined word?

   (A)   [d]
   (B)   [ð]
   (C)   [r]
   (D)   [θ]

For Question 12, listen as a student talks about a bicycle tournament.

The <u>event</u> was like, pretty huge, maybe like around four thousands bicycle, and then maybe people from another state come, and then this here, big <u>event</u> that we never had before.

12. The underlined word demonstrates the student's difficulty with which of the following?

   (A)   Word stress
   (B)   Consonant voicing
   (C)   Nasalization
   (D)   Aspiration

For Question 13, listen as a student talks about a trip.

Oh, yeah, uh, I was in, um, um, on <u>Niagara</u> Fall, on Niagara Falls.

13. In the underlined word, the student does which of the following?

    (A) Deletes a vowel sound
    (B) Adds a consonant between two vowel sounds
    (C) Adds a glottal stop at the end
    (D) Deletes a consonant sound

For Question 14, listen as a speaker talks about people in his country.

So there is a <u>huge mix</u>, but it is, it is very interesting.

14. In the underlined phrase, the student demonstrates difficulty pronouncing which of the following English phonemes?

    (A) /h/
    (B) /dʒ/
    (C) /ɪ/
    (D) /u/

For Question 15, listen to the student talk about studying.

I . . . I was studying in the, in the, in the school.

15. In the speech sample, the student demonstrates difficulty with which of the following?

    (A) Initial /ð/
    (B) Initial /s/
    (C) Rounded vowels
    (D) Voiceless stops

STOP

THIS IS THE END OF PART B
THIS IS THE END OF THE RECORDED PORTION OF THE TEST

Section I: Analysis of Student Language Production

Part C: Writing

Approximate time—7 minutes

Directions: Choose the best answer to each question and mark it on your answer sheet. The questions in this part refer to a number of excerpts from compositions written by ESOL students.

Question 16 is based on the following excerpt from a student's essay about a vacation.

I'm Nola. I go a new york and a philadelfia de las vacation. My familia is happy and I am happy. My hermana is happy and my tio like see my familia.

16. This writing example is characterized by which of the following?

   (A) Acculturation
   (B) Code-switching
   (C) Circumlocution
   (D) Ethnocentrism

Question 17 is based on the following excerpt from a student's essay about family.

The three most important people in my life are my mom, my dad, and my sister. My mom is important to me because she always understand me and she always help me. My dad is important to me because we always have fun together.

17. On the basis of the writing sample, this student has not yet mastered

   (A) third-person singular endings for regular verbs
   (B) simple present-tense forms of irregular verbs
   (C) use of adverbs of frequency
   (D) possessive pronouns

Question 18 is based on the following excerpt from a student's essay about a trip to a park.

I like the flower I like to see a animals cutes like squaro. I like to see a River in the Park and Enjoy the Spring.

18. The student's use of the word "squaro" is most likely an example of what kind of spelling?

   (A) Phonetic
   (B) Semiphonetic
   (C) Precommunicative
   (D) Invented

Question 19 is based on the following excerpt from a student's essay about teachers.

A good teacher is nice and caring. a good teacher is help in the class. also a good teacher is want to help the students. a good teacher is like help her students. a good teacher has alot pashents for the students. a good teacher is went is good with the students.

19. In this writing sample, the student's most prevalent errors involve which two of the following?

   I.   Capitalization
   II.   Plurals
   III. Formation of the present tense
   IV.   Adjective placement

   (A) I and II
   (B) I and III
   (C) II and III
   (D) II and IV

Question 20 is based on the following excerpt from a student's essay about people.

I like funny people. I think my cousin make me laugh and I think he's most funny person in my family. He likes to mimic people. I also like smart people. My friend Ivan is the smart person in the whold class. My mother is nice and she is kindest person I know. Sometimes my brother is help me, not always. My friend Julia is most loyalest person of my friends.

20. The writing sample contains several errors in the formation of

   (A) superlative adjectives
   (B) comparative adjectives
   (C) demonstrative pronouns
   (D) possessive pronouns

Question 21 is based on the following excerpt from a student's essay about frustration with friends.

When they don't do somethings that I told them not to do for more than a hundred times. This made me so angry because it's like they listen to me. My opinion are like nothing. Sometimes they do it because maybe just forgot. I don't even know I should be angry or not.

21. On the basis of the kinds of errors made in this excerpt, which of the following would be most appropriate for helping to improve the student's writing?

   (A) Circling errors and allowing the student to determine how to correct them
   (B) Directing the student to read the writing silently to herself to correct the errors
   (C) Instructing the student to read the writing to the class for peer editing
   (D) Reading the writing to the student and allowing her to listen for errors

Question 22 is based on the following excerpt from a student's essay giving advice to a new student in school.

I think the best advice is that join some after school club to let him ask questions about the school. We can also ask some student already in our school for a long time come to answer those question. Also to tell them something to be aware of and some thing or a few rule they might not know.

22. The most prevalent errors in the writing sample involve

   (A) number agreement
   (B) subject-verb agreement
   (C) verb tense
   (D) use of prepositions

THIS IS THE END OF SECTION I.
GO ON TO SECTION II, READ THE DIRECTIONS, AND
BEGIN WORK ON THE QUESTIONS IN THAT SECTION.

Section II: Language Theory and Teaching

Approximate time—60 minutes

Directions: Choose the best answer to each question and mark it on your answer sheet.

23. Which of the following kinds of assessment would be most appropriate for gathering information about what ESOL students have learned after completing a science unit?

    (A) Achievement
    (B) Proficiency
    (C) Diagnostic
    (D) Placement

24. All of the following are examples of minimal pairs EXCEPT

    (A) fare/fair
    (B) fair/care
    (C) fair/pear
    (D) fare/wear

25. Which of the following is the professional organization that hosts an annual conference for ESL teachers and publishes a quarterly research journal?

    (A) IATEFL
    (B) TESOL
    (C) ACTFL
    (D) NAFSA

26. Which of the following approaches to the teaching of reading and writing emphasizes meaning?

    (A) The linguistic approach
    (B) The Language Experience approach
    (C) The basal-reader approach
    (D) The sight-word approach

27. An ESL teacher is beginning a new position at an elementary school. The principal shows the teacher the existing textbooks available for use with ESOL students. Which of the following questions would be most important for the teacher to ask to determine the appropriateness of a textbook for use with ESOL students?

    (A) Do the units in the book provide sufficient practice tasks or exercises?
    (B) Are the students provided with an answer key to find solutions to hard problems?
    (C) Is the textbook published by a well-known and reputable company?
    (D) How much do the books cost per unit to replace?

28. Which of the following words contains a consonant digraph?

    (A) Shirt
    (B) Trunk
    (C) Pajamas
    (D) Extra

29. Which of the following transcriptions best represents the way a native speaker of standard American English would pronounce the word "these"?

    (A) [θiyz]
    (B) [ðiyz]
    (C) [ðɪs]
    (D) [θɪs]

30. Consider the following sentence: "He's a very creative boy." Which of the following best represents the stress pattern a native speaker of standard American English would use in pronouncing the word "creative"?

    (A) • • ●
    (B) • • •
    (C) ● • •
    (D) ● ● •

31. A nonnative speaker of English consistently pronounces "that" as [dæt]. This is an example of

    (A) phoneme substitution
    (B) choice of allophone
    (C) palatalization
    (D) voicing

32. Which of the following sentences is in the passive voice?

    1. Dmitry has been working nights.
    2. The train is due by 3 o'clock.
    3. Eva has passed her classes.
    4. Dinner is being prepared.

    (A) 1
    (B) 2
    (C) 3
    (D) 4

33. As a newcomer and beginning ESOL student, Yih Ming rapidly acquired irregular past tense forms such as "went" and "came." Shortly thereafter, she began to say "goed" and "comed."

    This development is best explained by the concept of

    (A) redundancy reduction
    (B) overgeneralization
    (C) phonemic awareness
    (D) L1 transfer

34. Which of the following are examples of bottom-up reading strategies?

    I. Activating prior knowledge to make predictions
    II. Drawing conclusions based on text structure
    III. Analyzing relationships between words in a sentence
    IV. Deciphering the meanings of individual words in a sentence

    (A) I and II only
    (B) III and IV only
    (C) I, II, and III only
    (D) I, III, and IV only

35. Which of the following approaches to language teaching involve the use of students' native languages during instruction?

    I. Audiolingualism
    II. Direct Method
    III. Suggestopedia
    IV. Community Language Learning

    (A) I and II only
    (B) III and IV only
    (C) I, II, and IV only
    (D) II, III, and IV only

36. Which of the following terms has been used by second-language theorists to refer to a point past which language learners cannot progress without exceptional effort or motivation?

    (A) Fossilization
    (B) Pidginization
    (C) Reduced speech
    (D) Information gap

37. An ESOL student demonstrates articulation problems in English. Before the teacher refers the student for a speech evaluation, it is most important to determine

    (A) how long the student has been studying English
    (B) whether the student is performing at grade level in reading
    (C) whether the problem occurs when the student speaks in his or her native language
    (D) the extent to which the problem affects the student's ability to be understood by others

38. Appropriate instruction for ESOL students with limited formal schooling (LFS) emphasizes

    (A) project-based learning and portfolio assessment
    (B) self-directed study in independent learning centers
    (C) visually rich classrooms and a focus on familiar experiences
    (D) pullout of such students for intensive grammar-based instruction

39. Ms. Phelps has complained that one of her ESOL students is disrespectful. The student never looks at her when answering a question. Which of the following responses by the ESL teacher would be most appropriate?

    (A) Suggesting that the teacher refer the student to the school counselor
    (B) Explaining that avoiding eye contact is a sign of respect in many cultures
    (C) Telling the teacher to insist that the student make direct eye contact when spoken to
    (D) Recommending that the teacher refuse to speak to the student unless eye contact is made

40. "Students from this country are the best spellers."

    "Students of this ethnicity have the best penmanship."

    The statements above are examples of

    (A) cultural diversity
    (B) personal observation
    (C) cultural awareness
    (D) stereotyping

41. Student portfolios, observation checklists, reading logs, and dialogue presentations are examples of

    (A) self-monitoring strategies
    (B) performance-based assessments
    (C) behavioral objectives
    (D) informal assessments

42. The journal *TESOL Quarterly* is most likely to contain which of the following?

    (A) Reports of current research related to teaching English to speakers of other languages in the United States and abroad
    (B) Sample lesson plans and thematic units for teaching English to speakers of other languages
    (C) Quarterly updates on changes to ESL standards in the United States nationwide
    (D) Helpful tips and techniques for teachers of English to speakers of other languages

43. Of the following, which is NOT a core standard in the *ESL Standards for Pre-K–12 Students* published by TESOL?

    (A) Social language
    (B) Academic language
    (C) Sociocultural knowledge
    (D) Explicit grammatical knowledge

44. Which of the following best describes the difference between a transitional bilingual-education program and a maintenance bilingual-education program?

    (A) A transitional program is designed for ESOL students, while a maintenance program is designed for heritage language speakers.
    (B) The goal of a transitional program is full bilingualism, while the goal of a maintenance program is maintaining English proficiency.
    (C) A transitional program pushes for English-language proficiency as soon as possible, while a maintenance program aims for full bilingualism and biliteracy.
    (D) A transitional program works with students from many language backgrounds, while a maintenance program deals only with students from the same language background.

45. Which of the following evaluations would most likely be used by a teacher following the Communicative Language Teaching approach?

    (A) A discrete-point test in which students are asked to complete sentences written in dialogue form
    (B) An evaluation in which students rate their own performance against a scoring rubric
    (C) An application evaluation in which students are required to transfer what they have been studying to a new context
    (D) An integrative test in which students are asked to write a letter to a friend

46. Which of the following programs is most consistent with the belief that English should be the sole official language spoken in the United States?

    (A) ESL inclusion
    (B) Developmental bilingual education
    (C) Dual immersion
    (D) Maintenance bilingual education

47. A middle school principal asks an ESL teacher to evaluate the English proficiency of a new student from Country X. After the assessment, the ESL teacher does not recommend any ESL services. The principal is surprised, given the student's strong accent. Which of the following provides the most likely explanation for the ESL teacher's decision?

    (A) The student used a different register with the teacher than with the principal.
    (B) The ESL teacher realized that the student's pronunciation would probably become understandable with more practice.
    (C) The ESL teacher recognized that the student spoke an acceptable variety of English.
    (D) The student's affective filter had kept him from speaking with confidence to the principal.

48. Which of the following is an example of invented spelling?

    (A) "Home" for "house"
    (B) "Bog" for "dog"
    (C) "Elafunt" for "elephant"
    (D) "Freind" for "friend"

49. A group of fourth-grade intermediate-level ESOL students are using the writing process to construct a paragraph. They have completed their first drafts and obtained a peer review. Which of the following are they most likely to do next?

    (A) Submit the final draft
    (B) Brainstorm
    (C) Proofread
    (D) Revise

50. Which of the following approaches to correcting speech errors is most appropriate to use with beginning language learners in a conversation class?

    (A) Correct as many errors as possible to prevent fossilization of incorrect structures
    (B) Refrain from correcting errors to avoid embarrassing students
    (C) Correct only those errors that interfere with communicating meaning
    (D) Refrain from correcting pronunciation errors but correct grammatical errors

51. Adeyinka is a newly arrived high school ESOL student. Ms. Verderi, a history teacher, approaches the ESL teacher with the following complaint: "Adeyinka is so disrespectful. He constantly disrupts class by calling out answers rather than raising his hand. What should I do?" Which of the following responses from the ESL teacher would be most helpful?

    (A) "Let him continue to call out answers. Responding in class will raise his self-esteem."
    (B) "Remind him to raise his hand. He may come from a culture that encourages spontaneous responses."
    (C) "Don't respond when he calls out. Acknowledging his responses will only encourage him to continue."
    (D) "Reprimand him. It's important for him to learn that he is breaking an established class rule."

52. Federal law requires that schools administer a home language survey to any newly enrolled student to determine whether

    (A) a language other than, or in addition to, English is spoken in the student's home
    (B) the student speaks enough English to exit ESOL services in the current school year
    (C) members of the student's family are literate in their first language
    (D) instruction is mandated for the home language

53. Which of the following would be the most effective way for a teacher to identify semantic and syntactic gaps in students' understanding of a topic prior to the beginning of a unit?

    (A) Asking students to memorize a list of vocabulary words related to the topic
    (B) Discussing students' prior experiences related to the topic
    (C) Having students read aloud from a book about the topic
    (D) Handing out a list of comprehension questions about the topic

54. Which of the following is an example of a metacognitive learning strategy that could be modeled for ESOL students?

    (A) Note taking
    (B) Group work
    (C) Self-monitoring
    (D) Translation

55. An ESL teacher is planning a lesson about clothing vocabulary for beginning students. First, he will play a tape of two students talking about buying some clothes. Next, the teacher will distribute a page with the taped dialogue written out; the students will be asked to repeat the dialogue several times as the teacher models it. The homework assignment will be to memorize the dialogue for class the next day.

Which of the following methods of instruction is the teacher using?

(A) Total Physical Response
(B) Suggestopedia
(C) Audiolingualism
(D) Community Language Learning

56. The No Child Left Behind legislation has had a significant impact on the education of students having limited English proficiency (LEP). The impact can be characterized by all of the following EXCEPT

(A) annual assessment of LEP students' proficiency and progress in English
(B) an increase in the number of bilingual services to LEP students
(C) an increase in state and local accountability for LEP students' progress
(D) annual assessments of the reading and math ability of LEP students as well as all other students

57. When writing lesson plans, many ESL teachers begin their objectives with the following words: "Students will be able to…" Which of the following approaches to language learning and teaching is best reflected in the use of this phrase?

(A) A proficiency-based approach
(B) A performance-based approach
(C) A production-based approach
(D) A psycholinguistic-based approach

58. An ESL teacher incorporates many test-taking techniques and study skills into her classroom instruction. Which of the following instructional approaches most often includes these types of activities?

(A) Content-area instruction
(B) Strategy-based instruction
(C) Form-focused instruction
(D) Performance-based instruction

59. Manuel, a nonnative English speaker from Costa Rica, has recently begun school in the United States. Although he has taken English courses in his native country and seems to understand spoken and written English, he performed poorly on the picture-prompt portion of an ESL placement test. In this portion of the assessment, he was unable to talk about or answer questions based on a picture showing children playing in the snow.

Given this information, the most likely reason for Manuel's difficulty with the picture part of the assessment is

(A) cultural bias in the test
(B) negative transfer
(C) a problem with the administration of the test
(D) poor-quality illustrations

60. Which of the following is the best explanation for why an ESL teacher may choose to assess students in both English and their native language?

(A) To determine language dominance and distinguish between issues of proficiency, giftedness, and learning problems for ESOL students
(B) To determine the first language of ESOL students and assess their comfort with code-switching between L1 and L2
(C) To assess the degree of transfer from L2 to the student's L1
(D) To evaluate dialectical variation in the student's L1

61. Which of the following criteria is LEAST likely to be important for evaluating the quality of a language-assessment instrument?

    (A) The instrument should be standards-based.
    (B) The instrument should be valid and reliable.
    (C) The instrument should be focused on a target grammatical form.
    (D) The instrument should be performance-based.

62. Which of the following is most important to consider when placing and exiting ESOL students?

    (A) National, state, and local mandates and input from the student's family
    (B) The student's social interaction skills
    (C) Performance on IQ assessments and the student's learning style
    (D) The cultural background of the student and his or her expressed desires

63. A middle school ESOL student who has been in the United States for two years is being discussed in a team meeting. It is noted that the student is still at the beginning ESOL level, has difficulty focusing on assignments, has poor recall, and displays several inappropriate behaviors. The teachers have checked the student's educational history, which indicates that the same problems were seen the year before. Which of the following would be an appropriate next step?

    (A) Wait at least six more months because the student has not been in the United States long enough to be evaluated for special education services
    (B) Send a letter home to the student's parents urging them to help stop the inappropriate behaviors from occurring
    (C) Develop a pre-referral intervention plan to improve the student's classroom and study skills
    (D) Refer the student to the special education team and ask for testing and a physiological evaluation

64. During a planning meeting a third-grade teacher voices a concern about a beginning ESOL student who is not participating in class. The student arrived in the United States three months ago and still is not participating orally and is not interacting with other students. The teacher asks the ESL teacher for advice. Which of the following would be the most appropriate advice?

    (A) Design activities that require students to participate orally and interact with other students.
    (B) Understand that new students are often reluctant to participate and that more time is needed.
    (C) Refer the student for a special education evaluation.
    (D) Call the student's parents and explain that grades are based on class participation and homework.

65. Which field of study is concerned with the meanings of words, idioms, and nonliteral expressions?

    (A) Semiotics
    (B) Semantics
    (C) Morphology
    (D) Syntax

66. A middle school ESOL classroom recently received an unexpected visit from a local dignitary. The teacher did not have an opportunity to explain to the high-beginning students who the visitor was. Several of the students spontaneously greeted the official by saying, "Hey, what's up?" and "Hi, how's it going?" as he walked into the room. The principal overheard the greetings and later questioned the teacher about the lack of respect shown by the students. In response, the teacher devised lessons that explicitly demonstrated different kinds of social language, depending on the age and social status of the person being greeted.

    These types of lessons focus on the aspect of language known as

    (A) register
    (B) affect
    (C) abstraction
    (D) characterization

67. A sixth-grade classroom teacher approaches the ESL teacher for collegial advice. A student in her class is newly arrived from an English-speaking country, and the other students are making fun of the new student's accent.

    What advice could the ESL teacher offer to her colleague to help with this situation?

    (A) Plan after-school speech sessions to remediate the new student's pronunciation.
    (B) Suggest to all students in the class that they ought to speak more slowly and clearly in order to be understood better.
    (C) Use an adult volunteer to read to the new student and model the standard regional dialect.
    (D) Expose the class to others in the school who speak with dialectal variations and hold class discussions about the value of diversity.

68. All of the following are examples of scaffolding strategies EXCEPT

    (A) increased wait time
    (B) paraphrasing
    (C) dictation
    (D) use of visuals

69. Those who argue that students should be allowed to use their home language in class cite which of the following as the primary benefit of this practice?

    (A) It allows for review of grammar of the students' home languages.
    (B) It increases sociolinguistic awareness.
    (C) It exposes other students to the concept of home languages.
    (D) It enhances exposure to developmentally appropriate content.

70. All of the following are examples of teaching techniques that emphasize meaningful student interaction EXCEPT

    (A) asking students to perform tasks that require collaboration
    (B) asking students to memorize and perform a dialogue
    (C) having students read and comment on each other's writing assignments
    (D) integrating activities drawing on students' interests

71. An instructional activity that focuses on specific minimal pairs would assist beginning ESOL students primarily by

    (A) helping them distinguish between different sounds of English
    (B) familiarizing them with how native speakers interact in English
    (C) comparing English sounds to sounds present in their home language
    (D) centering their attention on English spelling patterns

72. Which of the following is NOT true of Cummins' cognitive academic language proficiency?

    (A) It is context reduced.
    (B) It is critical to success in formal educational settings.
    (C) It is needed to engage in social discourse effectively.
    (D) It takes longer to acquire than basic interpersonal communication skills.

73. The study of morphology includes all of the following EXCEPT

    (A) meanings of prefixes and suffixes
    (B) combining words to make new words
    (C) inflecting nouns and verbs
    (D) sound-to-letter correspondence

74. A biology teacher has expressed concern that intermediate-proficiency ESOL students in her classes are not clearly demonstrating their understanding because their writing skills are impeding their ability to describe the lab and its outcomes in lab reports.

    To enhance the quality of the ESOL students' writing in their lab reports, which of the following should the biology teacher do for both her ESOL students and their native English-speaking classmates?

    (A) Allow extra time to perform the experiments
    (B) Have ESOL students work in pairs during lab experiments
    (C) Model the correct style of a lab report
    (D) Allow extra time to submit the lab reports

75. All of the following statements are true of performance-based assessments EXCEPT:

    (A) They may be used for formative or summative evaluations.
    (B) They may include demonstrations or artistic interpretations.
    (C) They should not be used to assess content-area knowledge.
    (D) They can be used in place of multiple-choice assessments.

76. An ESL teacher seeks to build a classroom community by helping students get to know each other, creating problem-solving activities for students to work on together, and engaging students in projects with real-life applications. With which of the following is this orientation most consistent?

    (A) Behaviorism
    (B) Constructivism
    (C) Team teaching
    (D) Open classrooms

For **Questions 77–84**, each set of lettered choices below refers to the numbered questions immediately following it. Select the one lettered choice that best answers each question and then fill in the corresponding space on the answer sheet. A choice may be used once, more than once, or not at all in each set.

For Questions 77–80, choose from among the following four teaching methods.

    (A)   Audiolingualism
    (B)   Communicative Language Teaching
    (C)   Silent Way
    (D)   Total Physical Response

77. Utilizes drills and pattern practice frequently

78. Subordinates teaching to learning

79. Emphasizes direct association with the target language

80. Encourages interaction with others in the target language

Questions 81–84 refer to the following four class activities designed for a high school ESL class.

    (A)   Imagine that your friend has never made a paper airplane. Explain to your friend how to make one. Now explain the same thing to a 4-year-old child.
    (B)   Explain how changing the sentence "It's mine" to "It's mine?" changes the meaning of the sentence.
    (C)   Study the ten words on the board that have plural endings. What rule can you think of that explains how to add plural endings to these kinds of words?
    (D)   Based on what we have studied in class so far, put these rocks into one of the bins labeled "igneous," "metamorphic," and "sedimentary."

81. Which activity primarily asks students to identify and classify?

82. Which activity focuses specifically on students' development of metalinguistic awareness?

83. Which activity asks students to interpret paralinguistic features of communication?

84. Which activity focuses on students' ability to switch registers?

Question 85 refers to the following pairs of words.

who's	→	whose
sun	→	son
feet	→	feat

85. The words in the two columns above can best be described as

    (A) antonyms
    (B) synonymns
    (C) homophones
    (D) allophones

86. Most two-way bilingual ESL programs in the United States are conducted in Spanish and English primarily because

    (A) Federal legislation supports two-way bilingual programs that feature Spanish language instruction.
    (B) There are not as many qualified teachers and paraprofessionals to support two-way bilingual programs in other languages.
    (C) English-speaking students are more likely to use Spanish, rather than other non-English languages, outside of school.
    (D) Two-way immersion works most effectively when the two languages share commonalities, as Spanish and English do.

87. A native speaker of English would be most likely to use a rising intonation at the end of which of the following utterances?

    (A) "Would you like coffee?"
    (B) "I'm from Wisconsin."
    (C) "He switched with Elizabeth."
    (D) "Do you want it short or long?"

88. Gina is from the United States, and Ivanny is a student recently arrived from Brazil. As Ivanny leaves the classroom one day, she shouts to Gina, "Call me tonight!" Gina responds with an "OK" sign with her thumb and index finger forming a circle to indicate that she has heard the request. Ivanny becomes upset and says she will not answer the phone. The next day Gina and Ivanny are not speaking to each other. Which of the following would be most important for the teacher to consider when speaking to the two students initially?

    (A) Nonverbal communication can be as significant as verbal communication.
    (B) Cross-cultural friendships can be difficult to maintain.
    (C) Culture shock can affect recently arrived students for several months.
    (D) Telephone conversations can be difficult for second-language learners.

89. Which of the following best characterizes Krashen's recommendations for determining appropriateness of reading materials for ESL learners?

    (A) They should be selected on the basis of grammatical structures that have already been taught.
    (B) They should be chosen by individual students regardless of the students' language ability and text difficulty.
    (C) They should be selected by teachers based on an assessment of students' abilities.
    (D) They should be at a level of complexity slightly beyond the reader's current reading level.

90. The implication of the United States Supreme Court decision in *Lau* v. *Nichols* is that in order to ensure that students who are nonnative speakers of English participate effectively in an educational program, they should

    (A) receive bilingual education
    (B) receive instruction in basic English skills
    (C) be given pullout ESL classes
    (D) get equal numbers of textbooks and other resources

Chapter 6
Right Answers and Explanations

▶   ▶   ▶   ▶   ▶   ▶   ▶   ▶   ▶   ▶   ▶   ▶

Now that you have answered all of the practice questions, you can check your work. Compare your answers to the multiple-choice questions with the correct answers in the table below.

Question Number	Correct Answer	Content Category
1	D	Analysis of Student Language Production; Linguistic Theory: Syntax
2	A	Analysis of Student Language Production; Linguistic Theory: Syntax
3	B	Analysis of Student Language Production; Linguistic Theory: Syntax
4	B	Analysis of Student Language Production; Linguistic Theory: Psycholinguistics
5	B	Analysis of Student Language Production; Linguistic Theory: Syntax
6	C	Analysis of Student Language Production; Linguistic Theory: Psycholinguistics
7	A	Analysis of Student Language Production; Linguistic Theory: Syntax
8	A	Analysis of Student Language Production; Linguistic Theory: Phonology
9	D	Analysis of Student Language Production; Linguistic Theory: Phonology
10	A	Analysis of Student Language Production; Linguistic Theory: Phonology
11	C	Analysis of Student Language Production; Linguistic Theory: Phonology
12	A	Analysis of Student Language Production; Linguistic Theory: Phonology
13	A	Analysis of Student Language Production; Linguistic Theory: Phonology
14	C	Analysis of Student Language Production; Linguistic Theory: Phonology
15	B	Analysis of Student Language Production; Linguistic Theory: Phonology
16	B	Analysis of Student Language Production; Linguistic Theory: Psycholinguistics
17	A	Analysis of Student Language Production; Linguistic Theory: Syntax
18	D	Analysis of Student Language Production; Linguistic Theory: Psycholinguistics
19	B	Analysis of Student Language Production; Linguistic Theory: Syntax
20	A	Analysis of Student Language Production; Linguistic Theory: Syntax

Question Number	Correct Answer	Content Category
21	D	Analysis of Student Language Production; Teaching Methods and Techniques
22	A	Analysis of Student Language Production; Linguistic Theory: Syntax
23	A	Teaching Methods and Techniques
24	A	Linguistic Theory: Phonology
25	B	Professional Issues: Curriculum and Materials
26	B	Teaching Methods and Techniques
27	A	Professional Issues: Curriculum and Materials
28	A	Teaching Methods and Techniques
29	B	Linguistic Theory: Phonology
30	D	Linguistic Theory: Phonology
31	A	Linguistic Theory: Phonology
32	D	Linguistic Theory: Syntax
33	B	Linguistic Theory: Psycholinguistics
34	B	Teaching Methods and Techniques
35	B	Teaching Methods and Techniques
36	A	Linguistic Theory: Psycholinguistics
37	C	Assessment Techniques and Cultural Issues: Evaluation and Assessment
38	C	Teaching Methods and Techniques; Professional Issues: Curriculum and Materials
39	B	Assessment Techniques and Cultural Issues: Cultural Issues
40	D	Assessment Techniques and Cultural Issues: Cultural Issues
41	B	Assessment Techniques and Cultural Issues: Evaluation and Assessment
42	A	Professional Issues: Curriculum and Materials
43	D	Professional Issues: Curriculum and Materials
44	C	Professional Issues: Programs and Models
45	D	Assessment Techniques and Cultural Issues: Evaluation and Assessment
46	A	Professional Issues: Programs and Models

Question Number	Correct Answer	Content Category
47	C	Assessment Techniques and Cultural Issues: Cultural Issues
48	C	Linguistic Theory: Psycholinguistics
49	D	Teaching Methods and Techniques
50	C	Teaching Methods and Techniques
51	B	Assessment Techniques and Cultural Issues: Cultural Issues
52	A	Teaching Methods and Techniques
53	B	Teaching Methods and Techniques
54	C	Teaching Methods and Techniques
55	C	Professional Issues: Programs and Models
56	B	Professional Issues: Curriculum and Materials
57	B	Professional Issues: Curriculum and Materials
58	B	Assessment Techniques and Cultural Issues: Evaluation and Assessment
59	A	Assessment Techniques and Cultural Issues: Evaluation and Assessment
60	A	Assessment Techniques and Cultural Issues: Evaluation and Assessment
61	C	Assessment Techniques and Cultural Issues: Evaluation and Assessment
62	A	Assessment Techniques and Cultural Issues: Evaluation and Assessment
63	C	Assessment Techniques and Cultural Issues: Cultural Issues
64	B	Linguistic Theory: Psycholinguistics
65	B	Linguistic Theory: Sociolinguistics
66	A	Teaching Methods and Techniques

Question Number	Correct Answer	Content Category
67	D	Linguistic Theory: Sociolinguistics
68	C	Professional Issues: Curriculum and Materials
69	D	Teaching Methods and Techniques
70	B	Teaching Methods and Techniques
71	A	Linguistic Theory: Phonology
72	C	Linguistic Theory: Syntax
73	D	Linguistic Theory: Morphology
74	C	Teaching Methods and Techniques
75	C	Assessment Techniques and Cultural Issues: Evaluation and Assessment
76	B	Teaching Methods and Techniques
77	A	Teaching Methods and Techniques
78	C	Teaching Methods and Techniques
79	D	Teaching Methods and Techniques
80	B	Teaching Methods and Techniques
81	D	Teaching Methods and Techniques
82	C	Linguistic Theory: Psycholinguistics
83	B	Linguistic Theory: Syntax
84	A	Linguistic Theory: Sociolinguistics
85	C	Linguistic Theory: Phonology
86	B	Professional Issues: Curriculum and Materials
87	A	Linguistic Theory: Phonology
88	A	Assessment Techniques and Cultural Issues: Cultural Issues
89	D	Teaching Methods and Techniques
90	B	Professional Issues: Curriculum and Materials

Explanations of Right Answers

1. This question tests your knowledge of the structures used for making comparisons. Here, the student has attempted to use elements of the comparative phrase "the same X like me" where "as X as me" would have been the more appropriate choice. Therefore, (D) is the correct answer.

2. This question asks you to identify a grammatical error the student makes in this utterance. The student's speech sample lacks a preposition (as well as an article) in the phrase "to go Internet, search." (A) is therefore the correct answer.

3. This question asks you to apply your understanding of verb tenses to decipher a student's utterance. The student refers to the past in two different ways: "when I have twelve years" and "for eight months." The first of these phrases is intended to indicate how old the student was when he visited the United States. The second phrase describes how long he stayed in the United States when he was twelve years old. The correct answer, therefore, is (B).

4. This question tests your knowledge of linguistic theory. In English, a verb that expresses a state of being (e.g., "I am") is used to indicate the age of a person, whereas in several other languages, a verb that indicates possession (e.g., "I have") is used. The process of incorrectly applying structures from one language to another is called negative transfer. (B) is therefore the correct answer.

5. This question tests your knowledge of question formation in English. The student's embedded question, "how it can works," should follow standard question word order: "How can it work?" In addition, the student fails to omit the third-person singular ending "-s" in the presence of the modal "can." The correct answer, therefore, is (B).

6. This question tests your familiarity with characteristics of students' speech. In this sample, the student first attempts one pronunciation of the first vowel in the word "busy," then tries another incorrect pronunciation, and finally returns to what she recognizes is the appropriate pronunciation as she produces the entire word. The correct answer, therefore, is (C).

7. This question asks you to identify a basic grammatical error in a student's speech. The student does not attempt to use pronouns in this sample, and his use of the conjunction "and" to coordinate phrases is appropriate. However, the adjective "bigs" is placed after the noun it modifies, and incorrectly includes the plural "-s" ending. The correct answer, therefore, is (A).

8. This question tests your ability to recognize a student's specific pronunciation trouble spots. The student is able to produce initial [f] and [s] sounds, as well as final [s] sounds. She stumbles on initial [θ] sounds, however, producing what is more accurately described as [s] in this position. The correct answer, therefore, is (A).

9. Your ability to identify sounds in speech and recognize their phonetic transcriptions is tested here. The student pronounces the word "bright" not too differently from English "bring" with a velar nasal after the vowel. Therefore, (D) is the correct answer.

10. This question tests your ability to identify student speech errors. The student is having difficulty with the "cts" consonant cluster in the word "insects." Therefore, (A) is the correct answer.

11. This question tests your ability to identify speech sounds and recognize their phonetic transcriptions. Here the medial sound spelled "t" in the word "cutting" most closely resembles [r], since it doesn't have a clear stop articulation. Therefore, the correct answer is (C).

12. This question asks you to identify a pronunciation error at the word level, rather than the level of individual sounds. The student pronounces the word "event" with a stress on the initial syllable rather than on the second syllable. The correct answer, therefore, is (A).

13. Your ability to identify and describe student speech errors is tested here. The student makes a number of errors in pronouncing "Niagara," including dropping the final vowel. The correct answer, therefore, is (A).

14. Your ability to identify sounds in speech and recognize their phonetic transcriptions is tested here. In this sample, the student pronounces the vowel sound in the word "mix" as [iy], rather than the way a native speaker would pronounce it, as [ɪ]. The correct answer, therefore, is (C).

15. Your ability to identify and describe student speech errors is tested again here. The student's pronunciation error here relates to the word "studying": He adds an extra syllable to the beginning of the word to avoid a word-initial s-cluster. This error is common for students with a Spanish-language background. The correct answer, therefore, is (B).

16. This question tests your knowledge of both cross-cultural and linguistic phenomena commonly encountered in the field of ESOL. The student's writing includes phrases in English and Spanish, used fairly interchangeably. Code-switching is the term that most aptly describes this pattern of language use, so (B) is the correct answer.

17. Your understanding of basic grammatical terms is tested here. The student uses adverbs of frequency, possessive pronouns, and irregular verb forms correctly. There are, however, several places in the sample where the student has omitted the third-person singular "-s" ending from regular verbs. Therefore, the correct answer is (A).

18. Your knowledge of developmental stages in writing is tested here. The spelling error in this example is based on the student's own (and not a native English-speaker's) pronunciation of the word "squirrel." Students frequently pass through a stage where they invent, or approximate, spellings of words based on how they think the words are pronounced. Therefore, the correct answer is (D).

19. This question tests your ability to identify common errors in student writing. The student capitalizes the first word in only one of the six sentences in the sample. There are also several errors in the formation of the present tense: "is help," "is want to help," "is like help." The correct answer, therefore, is (B).

20. In this question, your knowledge of the formation of several different kinds of adjectives is tested. The writer is apparently trying to discuss several people who best exemplify different characteristics. There is evidence that the writer has an emerging understanding of the ways to form superlative adjectives, since both "most" and "-est" are used frequently but inconsistently throughout the sample. The correct answer is (A).

21. This question asks you to apply an appropriate form of error correction to a given sample of writing. A student at this level would probably most benefit from hearing the essay aloud since often there is greater mastery of oral language before written language. The correct answer, therefore, is (D).

22. Your ability to recognize basic grammatical concepts is tested here. The student's writing demonstrates awareness of agreement between subjects and verbs, and the verbs are generally well formed. For the most part, prepositions are also used correctly in this sample. However, the sample contains several phrases in which a noun and its modifier do not agree in number: "some student," "those question," "some thing," "a few rule." Therefore, the correct answer is (A).

23. This question tests your understanding of concepts in assessment. Achievement tests can provide information about how much students learned and retained from a unit of instruction. The other kinds of tests are more appropriately used for other purposes. Therefore, the correct answer is (A).

24. This question tests your understanding of a basic phonological concept. A minimal pair is a set of two words that differ from one another by only one phoneme. Options (B), (C), and (D) are all minimal pairs by this definition. Option (A) lists two words that differ in spelling only, but that share the same pronunciation. These two words are homophones. The correct answer, therefore, is (A).

25. Your familiarity with major organizations in the field of English-language teaching is tested here. TESOL is recognized both nationally and internationally as an organization committed to improving the teaching of English to nonnative speakers. The correct answer, therefore, is (B).

26. This question tests your knowledge of several approaches to the teaching of literacy. In the Language Experience approach, students orally relate their personal experiences to the teacher; the teacher transcribes these experiences, complete with errors, and then develops other reading and writing activities based on the transcription. This approach allows for the development of materials and activities based on student interests and appropriate to student comprehension levels since they are student generated—without particular attention being paid to form or error correction. Therefore, the correct answer is (B).

27. Your understanding of how to evaluate curriculum and materials is tested here. Although information on cost and publisher may be important for selecting new materials, to make a selection from *existing* materials an ESL teacher would do best to ensure that there are ample opportunities for students to practice and use new information presented in the text. The correct answer, therefore, is (A).

28. This question tests your knowledge of terms associated with the teaching of literacy. A digraph is a pair of letters that together are used to represent one sound. The consonants "sh" in the word "shirt" represent a single sound. The correct answer, therefore, is (A).

29. This question tests your ability to recognize phonetic symbols used in the transcription of speech. Option (B) correctly represents a word beginning and ending with a voiced sound, with a tense vowel in between. Therefore, the correct answer is (B).

30. Your familiarity with common stress patterns and intonation in speech is tested here. A native speaker of standard American English would place the greatest emphasis on the second syllable of the word "creative." The correct answer, therefore, is (D).

31. Your understanding of basic phonological concepts is tested here. The fact that the speaker consistently pronounces "th" as [d] rather than [ð] indicates that a substitution is being made at the phonemic level in the speaker's mind. (A) is therefore the correct answer.

32. This question tests your ability to recognize the use of the passive voice. A sentence is passive when the subject is acted upon by an agent that may or may not be named. In sentence 4, the dinner is being acted on by an unnamed agent. In sentence 2, by contrast, there is no agent. The correct answer, therefore, is (D).

33. This question tests your knowledge of typical phases in language development. The most common irregular past-tense forms are generally acquired before regular past forms. Yih Ming's switch to "goed" and "comed" indicates that she has learned a new rule for forming verbs in the past tense and has overgeneralized its application. The correct answer, therefore, is (B).

34. Your understanding of basic processes in reading is tested here. Bottom-up strategies are those that focus primarily on the actual words in a text, as opposed to a focus on general meaning in top-down strategies. Choices III and IV describe strategies that focus on words rather than overall meaning. Therefore, (B) is the correct answer.

35. This question tests your awareness of different approaches and methods used in language instruction. In both Suggestopedia and Community Language Learning, the students' first languages may be used freely during instruction. Therefore, the correct answer is (B).

36. This question tests your understanding of common theoretical terms in the field of second-language acquisition. Fossilization occurs when a language learner appears to get stuck at a specific stage, continuing to have trouble with the same structures and errors and making little apparent progress toward greater proficiency. The correct answer, therefore, is (A).

37. Your understanding of processes involved in the evaluation of speech problems is tested here. In order to determine whether a student has a real speech problem or simply speaks with an accent or is unfamiliar with the sounds of English, you must establish whether the student has the same difficulty in the first language. Therefore, the correct answer is (C).

38. This question tests your awareness of classroom practices appropriate for a specific learner population. Students with limited formal schooling will likely benefit from instruction that draws on familiar experiences and engages them visually, since they are likely to have relatively limited literacy skills. The aim in the LFS classroom should be to make the students feel comfortable with formal educational settings. The correct answer, therefore, is (C).

39. This question tests your understanding of differences in communication across cultures. In many cultures, it is considered more respectful to avoid eye contact with a teacher than to engage in direct eye contact. (B) is therefore the correct answer.

40. Your awareness of cross-cultural differences and of the need to respect diversity is tested here. These overgeneralizations about broad groups of students represent stereotyping and could lead to unfair expectations in the classroom. The correct answer, therefore, is (D).

41. Your knowledge of current trends in assessment is tested in this question. All of the items mentioned are tools used to measure student performance in the classroom; all of them utilize means beyond traditional paper-and-pencil tests. Therefore, the correct answer is (B).

42. This question tests your awareness of publications in the field of English-language teaching. *TESOL Quarterly* is a professional journal dedicated to disseminating research on topics of interest to individuals in the field of English-language teaching. The correct answer, therefore, is (A).

43. This question tests your knowledge of a significant professional document. While social and academic language, as well as sociocultural knowledge, are included as core standards in the TESOL ESL standards, the teaching of explicit rules of grammar assumes a more peripheral role. Therefore, the correct answer is (D).

44. Your understanding of the various types of bilingual education programs is tested here. A transitional bilingual education program works to build students' English proficiency and put them into mainstream classes as quickly as possible; a maintenance bilingual education program attempts to educate students in the majority language while also promoting the use of the native or home language at school in order to develop bilingualism. The correct answer, therefore, is (C).

45. This question tests your knowledge of a specific approach to language teaching. The communicative approach to language teaching emphasizes the skills that are used in real communication, rather than strictly academic exercises. Writing a letter to a friend is a communicative task that requires the integration of a number of different skills. Therefore, the correct answer is (D).

46. This question tests your knowledge of different types of language programs for nonnative English speakers. ESL inclusion assumes that the students will not speak their first language in class. This is most consistent with proponents of English Only. The correct answer, therefore, is (A).

47. Your awareness of characteristics of different varieties of English is tested here. World Englishes share grammatical structures and vocabulary items with standard varieties of English, albeit with significant local variations. A native speaker of a World English variety may use pronunciation that is markedly different from standard American English pronunciation, yet still have full control over English structure and usage. The correct answer, therefore, is (C).

48. Your understanding of developing literacy skills is tested in this question. Invented spelling demonstrates a student's developing ability to write words phonetically. In choice (C), the student's spelling captures the sounds in the word "elephant" but fails to use the standard representation of those sounds. (C) is therefore the correct answer.

49. This question asks you to identify the correct order of steps in the writing process. Before students can revise their first drafts, they need feedback about what changes to make. Once they have this feedback they should revise their drafts. Therefore, the correct answer is (D).

50. This question tests your understanding of appropriate error correction for a specific population of students. Students in the early stages of language production benefit most from judicious correction of errors that actually interfere with communication. The correct answer, therefore, is (C).

51. In this question you are asked to apply your understanding of cross-cultural differences. The student's behavior most likely reflects acceptable practice in his home culture. The correct answer, therefore, is (B).

52. Here you are tested on your knowledge of current government regulations related to the field of ESOL. The home language survey is a federally mandated questionnaire that schools administer to newly enrolling students to determine whether a language other than, or in addition to, English is spoken in the home. Therefore, (A) is the correct answer.

53. This question asks you to apply your knowledge of effective teaching practices. In a discussion of students' prior experiences with a topic, the teacher can identify specific gaps in the students' understanding and build them into the development of a lesson. (B) is therefore the correct answer.

54. This question tests your understanding of various learning strategies. Metacognition involves thinking about what one is learning; self-monitoring, or checking one's own comprehension, is an example of a metacognitive learning strategy. The correct answer is therefore (C).

55. Your ability to identify the salient characteristics of various methods of language instruction is tested here. The repetition and memorization of dialogues is a common practice in Audiolingual texts and classrooms. Therefore, the correct answer is (C).

56. Here you are asked to identify the implications of current federal educational regulations. Under the No Child Left Behind legislation, bilingual services and approaches were diminished. For example, the name of the U.S. Department of Education Office of Bilingual Education and Minority Language Affairs (OBEMLA) was changed to the Office of English Language Acquisition (OELA). The correct answer, therefore, is (B).

57. This question tests your knowledge of several different approaches to the teaching and learning of language. A performance-based approach measures progress in terms of what real-world tasks students are able to accomplish. Therefore, the correct answer is (B).

58. This question tests your understanding of various instructional approaches. Instruction that focuses on teaching students how effective learners approach classroom tasks is informed by research on the importance of mastering various learning strategies. The correct answer, therefore, is (B).

59. Here your awareness of issues concerning language assessment is tested. Cultural bias in testing occurs when a test taker's performance on an assessment is negatively affected by the inclusion of material that is culture specific. Manuel does not necessarily lack the language skills being tested; rather, he may simply lack the cultural knowledge of snow-related activities on which the prompt is focused. The correct answer, therefore, is (A).

60. Your awareness of language issues in assessment is again tested here. It may sometimes be difficult, if not impossible, to obtain an overall profile of a student's skills if testing is conducted entirely in English; the student may have trouble as a result of limited English proficiency or some other factor. A student's scholastic aptitude may be underestimated if testing is not done in the dominant language. Therefore, the correct answer is (A).

61. This question tests your understanding of criteria that are important in the selection of a language test. A test that is valid, reliable, and standards- and performance-based can be expected to measure students' language ability accurately. On the other hand, a test that focuses on a specific grammatical form would not necessarily be an accurate indicator of students' overall proficiency. The correct answer, therefore, is (C).

62. This question tests your awareness of issues concerning the placement of ESOL students. National, state, and local mandates will indicate what is expected of students who have completed ESOL instruction and what level of English competency will be required of them in mainstream classes. (A) is therefore the correct answer.

63. Your awareness of appropriate channels for evaluating the special education needs of ESOL students is tested here. Before ESOL students are referred for special education evaluations, pre-referral interventions should be attempted. Based on the response to the intervention, the student might subsequently be referred for special education. The correct answer, therefore, is (C).

64. This question tests your understanding of stages in language development. New arrivals frequently go through a "silent phase," which may last days, weeks, or even months. It is important to give students time to adjust to their new environment. Therefore, the correct answer is (B).

65. This question tests your knowledge of subfields within the field of linguistics. Semantics involves the study of meaning in words, phrases and sentences. The correct answer, therefore, is (B).

66. Your knowledge of sociolinguistic aspects of language is tested in this question. Age and social status of the interlocutors are among the factors that contribute to variations in linguistic register. The correct answer, therefore, is (A).

67. Your understanding of how to deal with dialectal variation is tested here. Nothing further should be done to single out the new student's accent; rather, an approach that emphasizes the fact that many dialectal variations of English exist would be most appropriate in this situation. Therefore, (D) is the correct answer.

68. This question assesses your awareness of ways to aid students' comprehension. Scaffolding strategies are actions that can be taken by a teacher to help students comprehend meaning. Dictation is sometimes used to assess comprehension, but it is not helpful in building students' understanding. The correct answer, therefore, is (C).

69. This question asks about an issue related to the use of home languages in the classroom. The use of students' home languages provides students with access to content that is appropriate to their developmental level. Therefore, the correct answer is (D).

70. Here you are asked to apply your understanding of the theory behind a pedagogical approach. Activities designed to create meaningful interaction are usually highly engaging and somewhat challenging. Of the activities listed, the memorization of a dialogue for performance is the activity that is least likely to facilitate meaningful interaction. (B) is therefore the correct answer.

71. This question asks you to apply your understanding of phonological concepts to classroom practice. By focusing on minimal pairs, or pairs of words that differ in only one phoneme, the activity would provide students with practice in discriminating between sounds that are distinct in English. (A) is therefore the correct answer.

72. Your knowledge of a prominent theory of language development is tested in this question. According to Cummins, Basic Interpersonal Communication Skills (BICS) is the type of language that is necessary for social interaction. The correct answer, therefore, is (C).

73. This question tests your understanding of one of the major subfields of the field of linguistics. The correspondence between sounds and letters would more appropriately be described as an aspect of the study of phonology. Therefore, the correct answer is (D).

74. This question asks you to select the best approach to improving students' writing skills. Both ESOL students and native-English-speaking students would benefit from becoming more familiar with the specialized format of a lab report, a type of writing to which they would not necessarily have been exposed in other instructional settings. The correct answer, therefore, is (C).

75. Your knowledge of current trends in assessment is tested here. Performance-based assessments are quite adaptable instruments and are often suitable measures of students' knowledge in content classes. (C) is therefore the correct answer.

76. This question tests your knowledge of learning theories. Constructivist views of learning focus on how learners make sense of new information through such means as problem solving, working together, and applying information to real-life applications. The correct answer, therefore, is (B).

77. This question tests your knowledge of characteristics of various language-teaching methods. The Audiolingual method makes use of drills and pattern practice, often out of context, to ingrain correct linguistic form. The correct answer, therefore, is (A).

78. This question again tests your knowledge of the characteristics associated with various language-teaching methods. The Silent Way espouses the idea that students should be encouraged to discover rules themselves with minimal teacher intervention. The correct answer, therefore, is (C).

79. Here your awareness of various language-teaching methods is tested. Through the association of actions with words in the target language, Total Physical Response attempts to bypass translation and instead help learners to make direct connections with the target language. Therefore, the correct answer is (D).

80. Your knowledge of the characteristics of various language-teaching methods is tested here. The goal of Communicative Language Teaching is to allow students to interact meaningfully with one another in the target language. (B) is therefore the correct answer.

81. This question asks you to select an activity that gives students practice with new vocabulary through classification and identification. Placing rocks into specific bins based on certain characteristics is such an activity. The correct answer, therefore, is (D).

82. Here you are asked to apply your understanding of the term "metalinguistic knowledge," or awareness of the features and rules of a given language, beyond simply being able to use them. Extrapolating a rule for adding plural endings to words requires metalinguistic knowledge. Therefore, (C) is the correct answer.

83. Your awareness of aspects of communication that are encoded separately from words is tested here. Changing the punctuation of the sentence "It's mine" from a period to a question mark changes the sentence from a statement to a question. The correct answer, therefore, is (B).

84. This question tests your knowledge of sociolinguistic features of language. This activity, which requires the speaker to accommodate the different needs of children and adults, involves practice with shifting registers. Therefore, the correct answer is (A).

85. This question asks you to apply your understanding of a frequently used term. Homophones are two words that sound the same and may or may not be spelled the same way, but carry meanings distinct from one another. (C) is therefore the correct answer.

86. Your awareness of two-way bilingual ESL programs is tested here. In such programs, the language used for instruction alternates. Because of current demographics, among both students and instructors, Spanish and English are by far the most commonly paired languages. Therefore, (B) is the correct answer.

87. This question tests your knowledge of intonational patterns in English. A speaker asking, "Would you like coffee?" would most likely use a rising intonation on the final syllable of the final word of the question. Therefore, the correct answer is (A).

88. This question asks you to apply your understanding of differences in nonverbal communication across cultures. Hand gestures and body movements that have a neutral or positive meaning in one culture may sometimes have a quite different, very negative meaning in another culture. The negative meaning of a hand gesture can override the positive message that is being expressed verbally. The correct answer, therefore, is (A).

89. This question tests your knowledge of one of the most prominent theories of second-language acquisition. Krashen is most closely associated with the idea that learner input should be based on language that is slightly beyond the learner's current receptive level. The correct answer, therefore, is (D).

90. This question tests your understanding of a key court ruling regarding ESL instruction. The rationale for *Lau* v. *Nichols* was that students need to be proficient in English to have equal opportunities for education. Therefore, if they come to school lacking basic English skills, they need instruction in those skills. The correct answer, therefore, is (B).

Chapter 7

Are You Ready? Last-Minute Tips

▶   ▶   ▶   ▶   ▶   ▶   ▶   ▶   ▶   ▶   ▶   ▶

Checklist

Complete this checklist to determine whether you're ready to take the test.

❏ Do you know the testing requirements for your teaching field in the state(s) where you plan to teach?

❏ Have you followed all of the test registration procedures?

❏ Do you know the topics that will be covered in each test you plan to take?

❏ Have you reviewed any textbooks, class notes, and course readings that relate to the topics covered?

❏ Do you know how long the test will take and the number of questions it contains? Have you considered how you will pace your work?

❏ Are you familiar with the test directions and the types of questions for the test?

❏ Are you familiar with the recommended test-taking strategies and tips?

❏ Have you practiced by working through the practice test questions at a pace similar to that of an actual test?

❏ If you are repeating a Praxis Series assessment, have you analyzed your previous score report to determine areas where additional study and test preparation could be useful?

The day of the test

You should have ended your review a day or two before the actual test date. On the day of the test, you should

- be well rested

- take photo identification with you

- take a supply (at least three) of well-sharpened #2 pencils

- eat before you take the test

- be prepared to stand in line to check in or to wait while other test takers are being checked in

You can't control the testing situation, but you can control yourself. Stay calm. The supervisors are well trained and make every effort to provide uniform testing conditions, but don't let it bother you if the test doesn't start exactly on time. You will have the necessary amount of time once it does start.

You can think of preparing for this test as training for an athletic event. Once you've trained, prepared, and rested, give it everything you've got. Good luck.

Appendix A
Study Plan Sheet

Study Plan Sheet

See Chapter 1 for suggestions about using this Study Plan Sheet.

			STUDY PLAN			
Content covered on test	How well do I know the content?	What material do I have for studying this content?	What material do I need for studying this content?	Where could I find the materials I need?	Dates planned for study of content	Dates completed

Appendix B
For More Information

▶   ▶   ▶   ▶   ▶   ▶   ▶   ▶   ▶   ▶   ▶   ▶

Educational Testing Service offers additional information to assist you in preparing for The Praxis Series assessments. *Tests at a Glance* materials and the *Registration Bulletin* are both available from our Web site: http://www.ets.org/praxis.

General Inquiries

Phone: 800-772-9476 or 609-771-7395 (Monday-Friday, 8:00 A.M. to 7:45 P.M., Eastern time)

Fax: 609-771-7906

Extended Time

If you have a learning disability or if English is not your primary language, you can apply to be given more time to take your test. The *Registration Bulletin* tells you how you can qualify for extended time.

Disability Services

Phone: 800-387-8602 or 609-771-7780

Fax: 609-771-7906

TTY (for deaf or hard of hearing callers): 609-771-7714

Mailing Address

ETS—The Praxis Series
P.O. Box 6051
Princeton, NJ 08541-6051

Overnight Delivery Address

ETS—The Praxis Series
Distribution Center
225 Phillips Blvd.
Ewing, NJ 08628